HOW TO STOP FREAKING OUT

The Ultimate Guide to
KEEPING COOL
When Life Feels Chaotic

Carla Naumburg, PhD, LICSW

ILLUSTRATED BY **Letizia Rizzo**

Workman Publishing • New York

Workman Kids
Workman Publishing
Hachette Book Group, Inc.
1290 Avenue of the Americas
New York, NY 10104
workman.com

Workman Kids is an imprint of Workman Publishing, a division of Hachette Book Group, Inc. The Workman name and logo are registered trademarks of Hachette Book Group, Inc.

Design by Daniella Graner
Cover illustration by Letizia Rizzo

The publisher is not responsible for websites (or their content) that are not owned by the publisher.

Workman books may be purchased in bulk for business, educational, or promotional use. For information, please contact your local bookseller or the Hachette Book Group Special Markets Department at special.markets@hbgusa.com.

Library of Congress Cataloging-in-Publication Data is available.

ISBN 978-1-5235-1824-1

First Edition October 2024 APS
Printed in Dongguan, China, on responsibly sourced paper.

10 9 8 7 6 5 4 3 2 1

CONTENTS

INTRODUCTION

Fall apart. Flip out. Flip your lid. Break down. Meltdown. Implode. Explode. Throw a tantrum. Lose your temper. Lose your mind. Lose your cool. Blow your stack. Blow a gasket. Come unglued. Go bonkers. Go ballistic. Go bananas. Go berserk. Wig out.

There are lots of different ways to talk about freaking out. That's because *everyone* loses control sometimes, and we all do it in different ways. Before we go any further, I want you to remember two things: 1) Freaking out is a totally normal, human behavior, which means, 2) The next time you freak out, it's not because there's anything wrong with you! It's just what humans do. So take a deep breath and let's keep going.

We're going to talk a lot more about all of this throughout the book, but first, it's time for a quick quiz.

QUICK QUIZ

What Does "Freak Out" Mean to You?

When you read words like **"freak out," "meltdown,"** or **"go bananas,"** what do you think of?

A. Stomping out of the room and slamming the door as hard as you can.

B. Screaming at a friend or throwing a shoe at your sibling.

C. Sitting quietly with tense muscles, a tight chest, and tears leaking out of your eyes.

D. Swinging your softball bat or hockey stick as hard and fast as you can as many times as you can.

E. Stressing out about who to apologize to and how to make everything better as fast as possible.

Answer: Whichever answer (or answers) you chose, you're right! Those are all examples of different kinds of freak outs.

We all go a little (or a lot) bonkers sometimes. And even though our explosions and implosions are super common and completely normal, they can make our lives harder in a bunch of ways. How?

- **Freak outs feel bad.** You feel out of control when they're happening, and when they're over you may feel tired, sad, confused, and ashamed.

- **Meltdowns can feel embarrassing,** especially when they happen in public.

- **Explosions can create stress and tension** in your relationships with your friends, parents, teachers, coaches, and other people in your life.

- Depending on your style of flip out, **you might get in trouble** at home, at school, with your friends, or in your sports and activities.

- Losing your temper, bursting into tears, or freaking out **rarely gets you what you want.**

That's the bad news.

Fortunately, there's lots of good news.

GOOD NEWS #1: You can understand why you lose your cool. It's not because there's something wrong with you or you're not tough enough or strong enough. It's because human brains are wired to freak out in certain situations. When you understand exactly what's going on, it all feels a little less stressful and a little less overwhelming.

GOOD NEWS #2: There are things you can do to feel more in control when everything seems confusing or overwhelming and you feel like you're about to explode.

GOOD NEWS #3: You can learn to freak out less and recover more quickly each time you go berserk or fall apart.

This book will teach you how.

Over the next few chapters, we'll explore everything you need to know to stay calm (or at least calmer) when things get chaotic, including:

1 What freak outs look and feel like and how to figure out if you're freaking out. (Hint: it's all about your F.A.R.T.s—but not *those* kinds of farts!)

2 Why humans freak out when our buttons are pushed, and what makes our buttons so darn pushable.

3 How BuRPing (but not *those* kinds of burps!) can make your buttons harder to push.

4 What to do when your buttons are pushed anyway and you're about to go totally bonkers. (Spoiler alert: quacking like a duck can be a highly effective way to not lose your temper.)

5 What to do after the inevitable explosion happens—because it will, and that's OK!

If that seems like a lot of information, don't freak out! (See what I did there?) Each chapter has tools like quick quizzes and questions, helpful truth bombs, and fun freak out facts that will help you figure out your own habits and tendencies, and help you make sense of everything you're learning.

Got it? Great!

Not so sure? That's OK, too!

Either way, by the time you're done reading this book, you'll have a whole bunch of skills and strategies that will help you lose it less often and make your life easier and more fun. Try not to get too frustrated if things don't seem better right away—these strategies can take a little practice to get used to, but they're totally worth it.

Let's get started.

Chapter 1

WHAT IS A FREAK OUT ANYWAY?

So, you already know that there are lots of different types of freak outs. Now it's time to figure out what it looks like when you flip your lid. I want you to think back to the last time you lost it. What do you remember?

Did you think of that time you were watching your favorite show and then your little brother stole the remote and changed the channel, so you called him a name, shoved him off the couch, and stole the remote back?

Or maybe you thought about a time you got so mad you hurled your stuffed animal across the room and knocked over a lamp? (Whoops!)

Maybe you remembered when your friend at school burst into tears in the middle of recess and ran off the field before you could ask what was wrong?

No matter what you thought of, specific examples are a great way to understand all the different types of freak outs. As you read this book, you might want to pause and think about examples from your own life. A great way to do this is to think like a fly. Imagine you were a fly on the wall, watching everything. What would the fly see right before you flipped out? What would it see or hear that would let it know you were freaking out? Jotting down some notes or ideas or sketches or scribbles is also a great way to think about what the fly might have seen.

One more thing to keep in mind: Sometimes it's hard to think about our freak outs because we end up feeling ashamed or upset. That's totally normal, and if that happens to you, just know that you can always take a break, take a breath, and keep reading when you're ready.

Oh, and if you can't think of any examples or you're not sure, that's OK, too! This Quick Quiz will help you figure it out. There are no right or wrong or better or worse answers in this quiz. The goal is to simply get you thinking about what happens when you freak out.

What's Your Flavor of Freak Out?

① It's minutes before your big recital. You just realized you brought the wrong sheet music for the clarinet piece you've been practicing for months. Your whole family and your best friend have come to watch you play. But without your music, you've got nothing. Your music teacher is going to be so mad at you and you'll die of embarrassment. Do you:

A. Stand in the back of the room, unable to think, move, ask for help, or do anything at all.

B. Start screaming at your dad. He was the one who forgot to remind you to check everything. It's his fault you're in this mess.

C. Run to the bathroom, lock the door, and try not to cry.

D. Kick your music stand and stomp off the stage.

E. Race around the recital hall, checking every single music stand for your copy, even though you know there's no way it could possibly be on any of them.

F. Breathe in and out slowly and find a friend who also plays clarinet. Maybe they have the music?

2 You totally spaced out during social studies. When your teacher calls on you, the whole class turns and looks right at you. You don't have a clue what she's asking about or what you're supposed to say. Do you:

A. Stare at your teacher in silence because you literally can't form words.

B. Tell the teacher that you were distracted by the kid sitting next to you who wouldn't stop snapping his gum.

C. Leap out of your chair and grab the hall pass as you rush out the door.

D. Slam your textbook closed, knock it off your desk, and mutter about how you never liked this stupid class anyway.

E. Try to distract everyone with the first joke you can think of and hope the moment passes.

F. Take a deep breath, count to three, and ask your teacher if she can please repeat the question.

❸ Your parents won't let you go to your best friend's sleepover because it's your grandmother's birthday brunch the next day and they're sure you're going to be too cranky after a late night out. All your friends will be there, and it's so unfair that you can't go! Do you:

A. Totally glitch out from frustration and anger and forget the entire speech you had composed in your head with all the reasons why you should be allowed to go.

B. Snarkily remind your parents that you don't get cranky because of the sleepovers, you get cranky because you have the meanest parents in the history of the universe.

C. Roll your eyes as you pick up your phone and start scrolling through social media.

D. Stand in the middle of the living room and scream about how it's not your fault if you don't make any friends and grow up to be the loneliest person who ever lived.

E. Apologize over and over again for every time you've ever been grumpy in the past and fall to your knees begging your parents to let you go *pleeeaaaasssseeeeeeeee.*

F. Go outside and get some fresh air to calm down. Come back inside and talk to your parents about how important this sleepover is and see if you can find a compromise.

4 Your best friend has been ignoring you all week. You know it's because the new kid in class has an enormous house with his own basketball court and a hot tub and your friend is trying to score an invite. Your feelings are hurt and you miss hanging out with your BFF. Do you:

A. Repeatedly walk up to your friend and stare awkwardly at him because the words just won't come to you.

B. Throw the basketball at his head as hard as you can during PE. That'll teach him.

C. Ignore him back. Ignore him so hard it's like he was never even born.

D. Wait until everyone leaves the gym, pick up a floor hockey stick, and whack it against the wall a bunch of times.

E. Say you're sorry, even if you're pretty sure you didn't do anything wrong.

F. Go for a quick walk around the block to chill out and then ask your friend if you can talk.

Answers:

If you got mostly A's: You're a **freezer**. Not the kind where you store ice cream (although that would be awesome), but the type where you tend to freeze up in stressful or emotional situations.

If you got mostly B's: You're a **fighter**. You tend to lash out at the people around you when you're stressed out or overwhelmed.

If you got mostly C's: You're a **flee-er**. You tend to check out, take off, or run away rather than deal with whatever's going on.

If you got mostly D's: You're a **flipper-outer**. You're likely to explode in tense or difficult moments.

If you got mostly E's: You're a **fixer**. You'll apologize (even if you didn't do anything wrong) and bend over backward to do whatever you can to make everyone else feel better, even if it makes things worse for you.

If you got mostly F's: You have some solid skills and strategies for not freaking out. That's great! And if you're not there yet, that's OK! That's what this book is for.

If you got a jumble of answers: That's OK, too. Lots of people freak out in different ways depending on what's happening, where they are, who's watching, and how likely they are to get in trouble.

TRUTH BOMB

You don't have to get an A+ in Not Freaking Out. You don't have to be perfect. Nobody is. If you get a solid B or B−, that means you're not freaking out 80 percent of the time, which is A+ AMAZING!

As you may have figured out from the quiz, even though there are about as many ways to lose your temper as there are people who have tempers, most freak outs can be grouped into five general categories: Fight, Flight, Freeze, Flip Out, and Fix.

THE FIVE KINDS OF FREAK OUTS:
Fight, Flight, Freeze, Flip Out, Fix

1. FIGHT:

This is one of the most common types of freak out. Something happens, and you lash out and pick a fight with someone. Maybe it's the person who did the obnoxious thing that upset you in the first place, or maybe you lose it at whoever happens to be standing in front of you right at that moment, whether or not they did anything at all. Either way, you scream or shout, or say something rude that you know will make them mad. Or maybe you turn your ice cream cone upside down on some stranger's head. (I know someone—*an adult*—who did that once!)

8

2. FLIGHT:

Sometimes when things get hard or scary or confusing, you just take off. You stand up and stomp out of the room. You literally run away. Or maybe you physically stick around,

but you disconnect and disappear into a screen, a show, or a book. You do whatever it takes to get away from whatever is going on—either with your body or your mind.

3. FREEZE:

This is when you can't move, can't think, and can't do anything at all. It feels like you've lost control of your body, like your feet are stuck in glue or your bones have turned into Jell-O. Sometimes it even feels hard to breathe. This is most likely to happen when something super surprising, unexpected, or scary happens. (Or anything involving a spider. Spiders are the worst.)

FUN FREAK OUT FACT   Lots of people are scared of spiders, but only 0.1 percent of all spiders are dangerous to humans. Scientists think that their creepy little legs and sudden, erratic movements freak us out because our brains can't predict where they're going to go next!

4. FLIP OUT:

This can look a whole lot like fighting, but the difference is that it's not directed at anyone in particular. Sometimes you just scream or slam the door or stab at your dinner  as if you were trying to kill it. You mumble angry words under your breath, crumple up your homework sheet, or hurl your video game controller across the room.

5. FIX:

Sometimes when you're overwhelmed with fear or anxiety or you're super confused, you focus on fixing everything as quickly as you can. You rush in to apologize for or take back whatever you said or did (even if you didn't say or do anything wrong!). Maybe you crack a joke or offer to share your favorite dessert that you really don't want to share or do whatever you can to just make everyone forget about whatever happened and feel better as fast as possible.

Fight. Flight. Freeze. Flip Out. Fix. Take a quick moment to think back to your answers to the quiz on pages 3–6, and what you know now about the five kinds of freak outs. Which style (or styles) of freak out seems the most like you? Maybe you're still not sure, or you can't pick out just one. That's totally normal—lots of people freak out in different ways at different times, and sometimes it feels like we're freaking out in more than one way at a time.

The Most Important Thing to Remember

Freak outs can look and feel very different for different people at different times, and even for the same person at different times. There's no right or wrong—the trick is just getting to know your style and tendencies!

Now that you know what a freak out looks like, the next step is learning how to figure out if and when you're freaking out.

Chapter 2

HOW TO FIGURE OUT IF YOU'RE FREAKING OUT

ne of the most important steps toward *not* freaking out is knowing when you *are* freaking out. It might seem like it's super obvious—it's whenever you're fighting, fleeing, freezing, flipping out, or fixing. But the truth is that it's not always that clear.

Let me give you a few examples:

EXAMPLE #1: Imagine you walked onto the playground and saw the school bully giving your little brother (or sister or best friend) a really hard time. You instantly feel overwhelmed by anger. Before you even realize what you're doing, you march over and insert yourself between the bully and your brother, and you tell them to back off in your loudest, strongest voice.

Quick Questions: Is this a fight? Are you freaking out? Or was this just you doing the right thing for your little brother?

EXAMPLE #2: Imagine you're doing your homework at the kitchen table. The math problems are tricky, so you call your best friend so you can work on them together. Just as you get on the call, your dad walks in and starts snapping about how you're not allowed to have screentime until you finish all your  homework. Instead of getting into it with your dad, you say goodbye to your friend, pack up your papers and calculator, and head upstairs to finish your homework in your bedroom.

Quick Questions: Was this you fleeing? Was it a freak

out? Or were you making a good choice to not get into it with your dad when you had homework to do?

EXAMPLE #3: Imagine your best friend is acting weird. You think she might be mad at you but you're not sure why. You hate it when this happens—it's the worst feeling in the world. But instead of asking your friend what's going on, you apologize for anything you might have done wrong and offer her the chocolate chip cookie in your lunch bag.

TRUTH BOMB

People might disagree about whether or not something is a freak out. Some folks might think someone is really losing it, while other folks might look at the same situation and think they're reacting reasonably. Sometimes it can be hard to know, and that's OK! Talking it out with someone you trust can really help.

Quick Questions: Were you fixing? Was this a freak out? Or were you just being nice to your friend when she was having a hard day?

In each of these scenarios, you probably weren't freaking out. In fact, you were probably responding in pretty reasonable ways. But if you had shoved the bully, slammed the door in your dad's face, or gotten down on your knees and begged your friend for forgiveness and promised to do her science homework every day for the rest of the year, well, those would probably be freak outs.

So, how do you tell the difference? How can you know if you're freaking out or not?

Your F.A.R.T.s can help you figure it out.

OUR FREAK OUTS ARE LIKE FARTS

OK, not that kind of fart. Geez. I'm obviously talking about the acronym F.A.R.T., as in the four signs that we're freaking out. It stands for **F**eelings, **A**utomatic, **R**eactive, and **T**oo Far. F.A.R.T. is a great acronym because farts and freak outs actually have a lot in common. Here are a few examples:

• Just like farting, losing your temper is a completely normal part of life. Everyone does it (even though some people try to pretend they don't).

• Both farts and freak outs can happen when too much pressure builds up inside us.

• While we can make some changes that might help us fart and freak out less, it's still going to happen sometimes—and that's OK!

15

• The good news is that if we notice our farts and freak outs are coming, we can take steps to lessen their impact. (Going into another room is a great start in either situation!)

   • And most important, farts are HILARIOUS and the more we can laugh at how ridiculous life can be, the easier it all feels. The same is true when we freak out. It happens to all of us, and there's no reason to beat yourself up about it.

FUN FREAK OUT FACT Most people fart about fourteen to twenty-two times per day! Fortunately, most of us don't freak out quite as often.

Once you stop making fart noises with your armpits (don't worry, I'll wait!), it's time to talk about the four features of freak outs, aka F.A.R.T.s.

F IS FOR FEELINGS. Freak outs almost always come from big feelings, like anger, sadness, anxiety, confusion, embarrassment, or shame. Even big happy feelings can push you into a freak out sometimes. (Remember the last time you laughed until you cried? That might have been a freak out, too!) Sometimes you know you're having big feelings, but you still can't calm down. Other times you have no clue what you're feeling, or that you're even having a feeling, and it seems like the freak out came out of nowhere. This might sound weird, but it's really common and totally normal to have big feelings without realizing you're having them. Either way, the thing to remember is that your explosions are emotional (based on your feelings), not rational (based on facts and logic).

Our feelings are often the first part of our freak out, meaning the place where they start. But our meltdowns aren't only about our feelings; they're also about our behaviors—meaning how we act and what we do. And when we lose it, our behaviors are usually *automatic, reactive,* and *too much*—they're the *art* of the F.A.R.T.

A IS FOR AUTOMATIC. Most of us don't plan to come unglued. It's not like we come home from school, drop our backpacks on the floor, look around the house, and think to ourselves, "Well, Self, this seems like the perfect moment to completely lose it." It would be kind of awesome if that's how it happened, because then we could choose *not* to blow up. Sadly, it doesn't work that way. Freak outs can happen so fast it feels more like a switch has been flipped or a button has been pushed. Fortunately, when we learn how

to notice that we're on the verge of an epic meltdown, there are things we can do right then and there that will help us calm down and not lose it. Or at least not lose it quite so badly.

R IS FOR REACTIVE. The word "reactive" can mean two different things. First, it's what we say or do *in reaction* to something that's happening, like your parents nagging you about your science project or your sister stealing the last cupcake that was totally yours. Something has to happen to get you to freak out; it doesn't come out of nowhere. Sometimes the reason for your reaction is super-duper clear, like when that kid at school smashed the clay sculpture you'd been working on for weeks. Other times, you might have no clue why you flipped your lid; maybe your grandfather is moving in with your family and you didn't realize how stressed you were about it until you went completely bonkers at your mom for asking you to put away your sneakers.

But "reactive" is also about our ability to act quickly in response to danger—either real danger or something that seems like it might be dangerous. This is exactly what human bodies and brains developed to do, because our brain's Number One Job is to keep us alive. It can also help us tie our shoelaces,

memorize the capital city of every state, or even remember to take out the garbage. But at the end of the day (or even the beginning), our brains are focused on protecting us.

Here's an example: Each time you see a long, thin, squiggly thing on the ground and you're not quite sure what it is, your brain is more likely to think it's a snake instead of a stick and tell your body to jump out of the way. That's what your brain was designed to do, and it's an awesome response when the squiggly thing really is a snake because, yay, no snake bite! But when it's just a stick, you've freaked out for no good reason. But your nervous system can't always figure out the difference between actual threats and minor problems or no problems at all, which is why you sometimes have a big old freak out even when there's no real danger.

Your nervous system includes your brain, your spinal cord (which runs down the center of your spine in your back), and the nerves all over your body. There are more nerve cells in your body than there are stars in the entire Milky Way galaxy, and they can send messages that travel faster than 220 miles per hour, which explains why your freak outs can come on so freaking fast!

T IS FOR TOO FAR. Sometimes things happen that deserve a big reaction. Maybe your little cousin was about to run into traffic, so you screamed at him to stop and then you grabbed his arm a bit harder than you meant to, and he got scared and started crying. Even though the moment had all the features of a freak out—you had *feelings* (probably fear!) and you *reacted automatically*—you weren't actually losing it. Your reaction was totally appropriate given what was happening. Your nervous system did what it was designed to do in a potentially dangerous situation, and once you knew your cousin was safe, you probably calmed down fairly quickly.

Freak outs are different. Freak outs are when you go Too Far. Your reactions are more intense and more emotional than they need to be in response to whatever's going on. Maybe you exploded at your father when he asked you to set the table, even though it was your turn. Or you burst into tears at the mere thought of studying for your spelling test, even though it's only one worksheet. The situation feels out of control, you feel out of control, and your behavior is surprising and confusing and doesn't really make sense to you. And instead of everything calming down once it's all over, you probably still feel a little stressed and overwhelmed.

Feelings   Automatic   Reactive   Too Far

The trick is learning how to pause and calm down before you go TOO FAR. You can be angry, confused, or scared in many situations and still not go totally bananapants.

The Most Important Thing to Remember

You can—and will—have big, intense, unpleasant feelings. There's nothing wrong with that. The trick is knowing how to feel those feelings and manage them without going berserk.

Understanding why you freak out—and what your brain and nervous system have to do with all of it—is the next step.

WHY DO WE FREAK OUT?

If freaking out feels so bad, and isn't something we *want* to do, why do we keep doing it?

A. We don't keep doing it. We never do it. What are you talking about? Is it snack time yet?

B. We're not patient enough, strong enough, or smart enough to stay calm.

C. It's everyone else's fault. If people weren't so annoying, we wouldn't freak out.

D. It's just part of being human.

Answer: If you picked D, you're right. Go get yourself a snack, and then come right back so we can talk about all the reasons we keep freaking out even though it's not what we want to do.

There are lots of reasons why people go totally bonkers in confusing or chaotic situations. Here are the five big ones: **FREAK OUT REASON #1: Nobody ever taught you how to *not* freak out.** Ever since you started school, you've learned the alphabet, arithmetic, and maybe even the capital of Alabama. (It's Montgomery, in case you forgot.) This information will serve you well throughout your life. And maybe your parents taught you how to brush your teeth, empty the dishwasher, and feed the cat. These are all excellent life skills, too, whether you feel like doing them or not.

FUN FELINE FREAK OUT FACT Cats purr when they're happy, but they also purr to calm down when they're stressed. The next time you're feeling like freaking out, try purring. If it's good enough for Tiger, it might be good enough for you!

But there also a few things many of us haven't been taught yet, like advanced physics (rarely useful), how to drive a car (super useful), and why we freak out sometimes and how to freak out less (insanely, unbelievably, off-the-charts useful).

Fortunately for you and everyone else who reads this book, you're about to learn all of that. (Well, except for the parts about physics or driving. Sorry 'bout that.)

FREAK OUT REASON #2: You've had a lot of practice freaking out. As your Spanish teacher or basketball coach may have told you a bazillion times, the more you practice something, the better you'll get at it. What they probably didn't tell you is that you're *always* practicing something,

even if it isn't something you want to get better at. Pick your nose every single night? You're gonna be super good at it. Flip your lid every time your sister does something that annoys you? You'll be an expert lid-flipper before you know it! Fortunately, the flip side (pun fully intended) of that is also true—the more you practice calming down instead of blowing up, the better you'll be at that, too!

FREAK OUT REASON #3: Sometimes freaking out feels kind of good. I know I said that blowing your stack feels bad, and that's almost always true. But sometimes when your feelings get too big and your stress gets too tense

and your muscles get too tight, screaming, shouting, crying, or throwing things can actually feel good! It's common to feel relieved and even a little calmer when you finally get your feelings out instead of trying to hold them in. The trick, of course, is to figure out how to express yourself and get all those big feelings out without going Too Far.

FREAK OUT REASON #4: People in your life freak out a lot. You may know someone who loses their temper a lot—whether it's at home, at school, on the field, or in the supermarket. And just like you learned to speak by listening to or watching and copying the folks around you, you might also have picked up some of your freak out tendencies from the people you spend the most time with.

FREAK OUT REASON #5: **Our brains are wired to go bonkers when our buttons are pushed.** Everyone has invisible buttons that are directly connected to the fight, flight, freeze, flip out, and fix centers of their nervous systems. And just like pens were designed to write and pools were meant to be swum in, human brains and bodies are literally wired to freak out when someone or something pushes those buttons and they get overwhelmed, upset, scared, or stressed out.

Your buttons are kind of like an invisible connection between the people and things that happen in your life and how you feel and what you think about them—even if you're not aware of what you're thinking and feeling!

Let's say, for example, that you had a growth spurt over the summer. Or maybe you're the only one in your grade who didn't. Either way, when you walk into class on the first day of school, you're way taller or way shorter than everyone else—and you are *not* a fan of standing out. So you take a deep breath and head straight to your seat, hoping no one will notice.

But someone does notice, and they say something. Something that's supposed to be a joke, but it's not a nice one or even a particularly funny one, and you freak out. Depending on your style, maybe you knock their books to the floor or say something mean back to them or maybe your eyes well up with tears.

Whether or not you realized it, you had a button about your height, and when buttons get pushed, you tend to freak out *because that's what your brain is wired to do.*

FUN FREAK OUT FACT

The phrase "pushing buttons" comes from the 1920s, when appliances that could wash clothes and dishes and cook food at the push of a button were first invented. You push a button on the washing machine and ta-da! Your favorite sweatshirt is clean. You push a button on the microwave, and bam! Your pizza bites heat up all on their own. Someone pushes your button and blammo! You lose it!

WHY DO WE HAVE BUTTONS AND WHAT DO THEY DO?

OK, so you have these invisible buttons that connect your nervous system and the outside world. Unexpected, unwanted, unpleasant, and unsafe people and experiences push those buttons, and when they push hard enough or they push enough times, they trigger your fight, flight, freeze, flip out, and fix reaction. Just like the start button turns on the microwave.

At this point, you may be wondering *why* do we have a button for freaking out? How is that helpful? When you think about how awesome human brains are (they did invent slime, laser tag, and the Mars rover after all), it might seem kind of weird that they can't do any better than freak out when things go totally bonkers. But once you know why your brain reacts this way, it actually makes sense.

Your brain is made up of lots of different parts that control different parts of your body. There are two parts of your brain that are super important to understanding your freak outs—the prefrontal cortex and the limbic system—so let's focus on those.

YOUR PREFRONTAL CORTEX:
THE PLANNER IN YOUR BRAIN

Take a moment and think through a typical day in your life. What are some of the things you might do that you need to think about or plan for ahead of time, and then focus on while you're doing them? Some examples might be:

- Picking out your clothes for the day and getting dressed
- Playing catcher in the softball game
- Designing a robot with supplies you found around the house

- Baking brownies
- Studying for a math test
- Choosing something from the menu at a new restaurant
- Learning your lines for the school musical
- Loading or unloading the dishwasher

As different as these activities are, they all have one thing in common: they require you to think ahead about what you have to do, and then do those things without flipping out.

There's a particular part of your brain that helps you plan ahead, figure things out, and stay calm as you do

Prefrontal
cortex

whatever it is you do during the day. This part of your brain is right behind your forehead and it's called the prefrontal cortex (or PFC for short). Your PFC helps you think ahead, make decisions, think clearly, and not flip your lid when things get hard, confusing, or overwhelming.

Your PFC helps you think through a school field trip and pack everything you'll need for the day. It helps you remember the water cycle, and reminds you to take a deep breath and keep your butt in the chair when you'd much rather be roaming the hallways. No matter what you're doing during the day, your PFC helps you **Plan ahead, Figure things out, and Calm down**.

TRUTH BOMB

If it ever feels like your prefrontal cortex isn't planning ahead, figuring things out, and calming you down as often as you'd like, it's probably because it's not. Your PFC is still developing and it won't be fully online until you're about twenty-four years old! As you grow and mature, your PFC gets better and better at helping you not freak out when your buttons are pushed.

Here are a few other things to know about your PFC:

• Even though it's not a muscle, you can think of it like one. While your PFC will continue to develop as you get older, you can also train it to get stronger, which is something we'll teach you to do in this book. But just like your body gets tired at the end of a long day, your PFC gets worn out when it has to work too hard for too long.

• When your PFC gets too tired or overwhelmed, it shuts down, which is why it can feel impossible to think clearly and stay calm and thoughtful after a whole day of following rules, listening to your teachers, and getting along with other people.

• Fortunately, there are things you can do to help your PFC recover—like getting enough sleep, exercising, and doing fun stuff (yes, fun counts!)—that will give your PFC more energy so you can make it through the day without losing it.

YOUR LIMBIC SYSTEM:
YOUR INNER SAFETY SQUIRREL

What do you remember about the last time you or someone you know freaked out? What happened? Did you, or they, shout at someone or shred their homework into a million tiny pieces? Did you, or they, run into the bathroom, slam the stall door, and burst into tears?

No matter what your freak out looked like, your PFC was too tired and maybe too overwhelmed to do its job. Another part of the brain—the limbic system—was in control. The limbic system is tucked away deep inside the middle of your brain and includes the amygdala, hippocampus, hypothalamus, and thalamus.

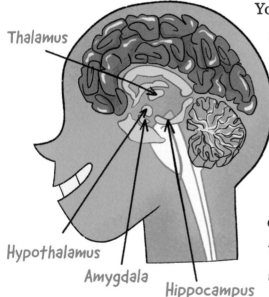

Your limbic system is responsible for a bunch of different brain functions, but its main job is to help keep you alive. It does this by constantly scanning the environment for anything that might be dangerous or scary. The limbic system also pays close attention to your big feelings and confusing thoughts, and it turns on your fight, flight, freeze, flip out, and fix reactions when it thinks they're necessary.

Oh, and one more important point about your limbic system: It's not wise or thoughtful. It doesn't carefully consider all the options or possible outcomes and then make the best, most reasonable decision. That's the PFC's job. Your limbic system is actually more like your brain's Safety Squirrel—the part of your brain focused on keeping you safe, no matter what else is going on.

Let me explain. You probably already know that squirrels are cute little rodents with big fluffy tails. What you might not know is that squirrels are quite clever. They have a lot of strategies for staying alive in the wilds of your backyard or neighborhood park. In fact, squirrels spend almost all of their time searching for food and keeping an eye out for predators and other threats.

The next time you're outside where squirrels hang out, try to notice what they do. You probably won't see them pull out a tiny pen and notebook and start studying their spelling words. Nope. In fact, chances are pretty good you'll see them:

• Stop whatever they're doing, and hold super still, aka FREEZE.

• Run off, either away from you or up a tree, aka FLEE.

• Defend their territory from other squirrels, which can turn into a FIGHT.

• Sprint around in an unpredictable pattern designed to confuse any predators that might be coming after them— kind of like FLIPPING OUT.

Now imagine one of those furry little guys with his tiny head and big fluffy tail, but this time, picture him wearing a tiny neon-yellow safety vest with a little whistle around his neck. (C'mon. How cute is that?) That little Safety Squirrel is kind of like our limbic system. The limbic system takes over in a few different situations:

1 When you're in—or might be in—a potentially unsafe or dangerous situation. For example, if you get lost walking home or you get stuck in a thunderstorm during the family camping trip.

2 When your limbic system gets confused and thinks you're in a scary situation, even though you're not. This usually happens when you get overwhelmed by upsetting thoughts, big feelings, and uncomfortable body sensations. For example, maybe you're feeling super annoyed at your classmate and your eyelid won't stop twitching and you can't stop thinking about your dentist appointment later. There's nothing unsafe happening, but all of these thoughts, feelings, and sensations happening at once might trick your limbic system into thinking there might be!

❸ When your PFC is just too exhausted and worn out to keep planning, figuring out, and calming down. When that happens, it just shuts down and the limbic system takes over.

When any of these things happen, our brain behaves more like a Safety Squirrel, doing whatever it can to keep you safe. Unfortunately, this often looks like a freak out.

Here are a few of the changes that happen in your mind and body when you go all squirrelly:

• **Your PFC shuts down and your limbic system takes over.** That twitchy little Safety Squirrel in your brain doesn't need to Plan, Figure Out, and Calm Down. It needs to FREAK. OUT.

• **Your heart beats faster and your breathing speeds up,** both of which send more oxygen to your muscles.

• **Your muscles tense up,** which gets you ready to fight or run away. If you're trying to hold still, you might start shaking or trembling, which is your body's way of staying ready for action.

- **Your vision changes,** and you might even notice tunnel vision, which is when your vision narrows and you can't see everything around you—kind of like if you were actually in a tunnel! This helps you stay focused on any possible danger.

- **Your stomach hurts or you feel like you're going to throw up.** This happens when your body moves blood away from your digestive system (which includes your stomach and intestines) and toward your muscles.

- **Your thoughts start racing.** It can become harder to think clearly or concentrate as your mind becomes focused on the threat and what to do about it.

These physical changes are designed to keep you safe, either by getting your body ready to fight or flee, and if you can't do either of those, then you might end up flipping out, freezing, or fixing instead. Just like some people are better at math and some people are better at languages, different people freak out in different ways. Oh, and if you don't remember anything like this happening to you, that's totally normal—it's really common to not notice your heart racing or muscles tensing while it's happening. Either way, the thing to remember right now is that when you're freaking out, your limbic system is in charge. That means your PFC isn't available to keep you from going Too Far, which is why you end up F.A.R.T.ing.

The Most Important Thing to Remember

Different parts of your brain are in charge at different times. It's much harder to stay calm when your PFC is offline and the Safety Squirrel in your brain is running the show—but it's not impossible!!

Now that you have a sense of what's going on in your brain each time you flip your lid, it's time to talk about your buttons and what they have to do with your thoughts, feelings, and freak outs.

Chapter 4

GETTING TO KNOW
YOUR BUTTONS
AND WHAT MAKES THEM LIGHT UP

Have you ever thought it would be pretty cool to be a robot? You'd have wires, processors, moving parts, and actual buttons that make you do something when they're pushed. Your wires would connect your buttons to your processors and moving parts, so you could roll across the floor or announce the time in Tanzania—

as long as you're powered up! Without enough batteries or being plugged in for a period of time, you'd be stuck in one place.

Sadly, you are not a robot, but you do have a few things in common with them. You have wiring and buttons that can make you do things when they get pushed. Your buttons are invisible, and instead of wires, processors, and parts, you have a nervous system, a brain, and a body. Your brain and nervous system (including the PFC and limbic system) are kind of like the wiring behind your buttons, and your thoughts, feelings, and physical sensations (meaning anything you feel in your body) are the electricity, or power, that makes your buttons bigger, brighter, more sensitive, and much, much easier to push.

There's one big difference between you and robots. Robots can only do what they're programmed to do, while you can be aware of what you're doing (or about to do), and decide whether you want to keep doing it or not. When it comes to freaking out, it stinks that it happens sometimes, but you can make choices. You can figure out when you're having a feeling or a thought, or when something is going on in your body that's making your buttons bigger, brighter, more sensitive, and easier to push, and then you can decide what to do next.

TRUTH BOMB

This may be the most important truth bomb in the whole book! Are you ready? Understanding your buttons—meaning learning what makes them bigger, brighter, and easier to push, as well as knowing how to make them smaller, dimmer, and harder to push—is the key to freaking out less.

Realizing when you're having an emotion, thinking a thought, or feeling something in your body is the first step toward turning down the power to your buttons and making them harder to push. It's not always easy or fun, but once you learn how to do it, it's kind of like a superpower. Even so, lots of people don't know how to do it. That's not because there's anything wrong with them; it's because unlike robots—which come with instruction manuals explaining how all of their buttons work—people aren't given instructions.

Until now.

A BRIEF INSTRUCTION MANUAL FOR HUMAN BUTTONS

Your buttons are powered by your thoughts, your feelings, and whatever is going on with your body in the moment. The bigger and more intense your body sensations, thoughts, and feelings are, the bigger, brighter, more sensitive, and more pushable your buttons get. And when those buttons are pushed often enough or hard enough, you freak out. If you can turn down the power to your buttons, they'll be harder to push and you'll be less likely to lose your cool.

The key to not freaking out is taking care of your buttons and making them as push-proof as possible. That means when you pay attention to your body, thoughts, and feelings, you have the ability to change your behavior—and not flip out.

We've been talking a lot about thoughts, feelings, and body sensations. Sometimes it can be hard to know what's a thought, what's a feeling, and how to understand what's going on in your body. Here are a few definitions and distinctions that can help you keep it all straight:

• **Thoughts, feelings, and body sensations** are the power behind your buttons, and they are **private** experiences. No one else knows what's going on in your body and brain unless you show or tell them, either through your words or actions. You can feel super sad or think your PE teacher is the meanest, most horrible person in the history of the world, or you can have a crazy sharp pain in your ankle, and no one will have a clue about any of it—unless you say it out loud or scrawl it across the whiteboard. Because saying and scrawling are behaviors.

• **Behaviors** (or actions) are different from thoughts, feelings, and body sensations in one really important way: They're **public**. Screaming, sprinting, slamming the door, and sticking your gum under your desk are all behaviors, even if nobody sees you do them. Freak outs are behaviors. Even freezing up can be a behavior, although it can be harder to spot. If you're not sure if something is a behavior or not, here's a handy test: if a camera in the corner or a fly buzzing around the room could see what you're doing, then it's a behavior.

Once you know the difference between private experiences and public behaviors, the next step is to sort out the difference between thoughts, feelings, and body sensations.

• **Thoughts and feelings often hang out together.** Sometimes we have a feeling that leads to a thought, and sometimes we have a thought that leads to a feeling. They can be hard to tell apart, but they're not the same thing. Even though thoughts and feelings both power up our buttons, it's useful to know the difference because we calm them down in different ways.

• **Thoughts live in your head.** They generally appear as sentences, like "Bananas are yellow" or "Today is Tuesday." You also have thoughts that describe your opinions about things, such as "Science is my favorite class" or "Ping-Pong is the greatest sport ever invented." Finally, you have thoughts that describe your feelings, which is not actually the same thing as having a feeling. Here's a handy test to help you figure out if it's a thought or a feeling: If you find yourself saying, "I feel *like*

_____" (emphasis on the word *like*), it's probably not a feeling, it's a thought. For example, you might feel mad, which is a feeling, but if you also feel *like* kicking your locker, that's a thought. The trick is making sure the thought doesn't turn into a behavior! Here's another example: You might feel anxious about your math test, which is a feeling, but you also feel *like* hiding in the school bathroom and ripping all

SOCCER IS MY FAVORITE SPORT.

I FORGOT MY RAINCOAT!

I CAN'T WAIT FOR ART CLASS.

the toilet paper to shreds instead of taking the test, which is a thought. (And if you acted on that thought, you might have gone Too Far, which would make your behaviors a big old freak out.)

• **Feelings live in your body.** Feelings aren't something you think; they're something you feel—that's why they're called feelings! They often show up as sensations in your body. Your jaw might tense up when you're angry, your stomach might feel queasy when you're scared, it might feel like there's something heavy on your chest if you're worried, or your eyes might tear up when you're sad. It can be hard to find the words to describe your feelings, but it gets easier with practice. Your body will give you useful clues, and finishing the phrase, "I feel _____" (without the *like*) is a great place to start.

headache

breathing hard

stress

racing heart

worry

TRUTH BOMB

There are almost one hundred feelings (or maybe more)! Common feelings that light up our buttons include tired, hungry, painful, happy, excited, angry, sad, worried, lonely, confused, overwhelmed, and misunderstood.

• **Body sensations** (also known as physical sensations) are anything you feel anywhere in your body. They might feel great, good, not so good, or downright awful. They can also feel neutral, which means something you notice that isn't pleasant or unpleasant—it's just there. Your physical sensations can include anything like a headache, a full tummy, a tight muscle, a twitchy eye, or a tingly finger. Sometimes it's really easy to notice what's going on in our bodies, and sometimes we really have to slow down and pay attention just to realize something's going on, like our heart is racing or our throat hurts, which might be a signal that our nervous system needs to calm down.

These are just a few explanations of how thoughts, feelings, and body sensations are all connected. Usually things are a little more complicated—for example, we might have several different thoughts or feelings at once, and we might have sensations in our body that we don't even notice! And sometimes it happens so freaking fast that we have no clue what's going on. That's normal, and we're going to get to some tricks and tools to sort it all out.

45

QUICK QUIZ

Thoughts, Feelings, and Physical Sensations: Which Is Which?

Can you match the phrase in Column A to the description in Column B?

A

A	B
My jaw is tense and my whole face hurts.	Thought
I feel angry.	Physical Sensation
I feel like I want to kick something.	Feeling
I feel like I might jump out of my chair.	Thought
My stomach feels like there are butterflies flitting around in it.	Feeling
I feel excited.	Physical Sensation

Answers: Your jaw hurting is a *physical sensation.* Feeling angry is a *feeling.* Wanting to kick something is a *thought.* Wanting to jump out of your chair is a *thought.* Butterflies in your stomach is a *physical sensation.* Excitement is a *feeling.*

One thing to remember is that people feel their feelings and think their thoughts in different ways. Some folks have very strong feelings that they feel all the time, while others don't have very intense feelings too often. Some people are often in good moods, while others tend toward cranky, anxious, or sad ones. People tend to think about different things, too—your twin might spend all afternoon imagining how to build a hoverboard while you're more likely to plan a surprise party for your best friend. There's no right or wrong way to think or feel; the trick is getting to know yourself, your body, your thoughts, and your feelings.

Quick Question: Take a moment to think about the people in your life— maybe your family members, friends, or even teachers and coaches. Does it seem like some of them feel their feelings more intensely than others?

How do you know? Do they talk about their feelings a lot, or wear their feelings on their sleeves? (This means you can often guess what they're feeling by the looks on their faces or the way they behave.) And maybe there are people in your life who rarely show their emotions, making it hard to know what's going on with them.

What about you? Do you feel strong emotions, or not so much? And do you often show what you're feeling? Maybe you're different in different situations or with different people. Maybe you express your feelings in big ways around your family, but not at school or around your friends. Again, there's nothing wrong with any of this; it's just good to know that different people feel things, and express their feelings, in different ways at different times.

Here are a few more things to keep in mind about your thoughts and feelings:

• **Your thoughts aren't always true.** You can think that elves are real or that you're the president of the universe, but neither are true, and they won't become true no matter how often or how hard you think them. The same is true when you have thoughts related to or based on your feelings. Maybe you're worried you won't get a part in the school play and so you think that you're a bad actor and will never realize your lifelong dream of performing

on Broadway. But those are just thoughts, and they're not necessarily true.

• **Your feelings, on the other hand, are never wrong.** They are always a match for whatever you're feeling in your body or thinking in your mind. Feelings aren't good or bad or right or wrong, no matter how good or bad they feel. They might feel awful, but just because something *feels bad* that doesn't mean it's *wrong*. You're always allowed to have your feelings—no matter what anyone else says. It's OK to feel frustrated with your parents or confused about your friendships or annoyed at your math tutor. It's OK to feel ashamed or sad or worried. It's OK to feel your feelings. Period! Whether or not you act on those feelings, whether or not you scream at your parents, blow off your friends, or flip out in the middle of tutoring, well, that's another story.

FUN FREAK OUT FACT Ever wondered what a "gut feeling" is? You probably know that your "gut" refers to your stomach and intestines. What you might not know is that there's a whole network of nerves around your gut, and they're connected directly to your brain. Sometimes we feel something in our bellies before we even realize it in our thoughts. So, the next time you feel something in your gut, don't ignore it—it might be telling you something important!

• **Every feeling has a beginning, middle, and end.** Just like your history class, it might seem like your feelings will last forever, but they won't. Feelings generally start out small, get bigger and stronger, and eventually calm down again—kind of like a wave in the ocean. Sometimes this happens so quickly it can be hard to see the whole journey, and it feels like you're just getting pummeled by the wave. That's completely normal. Just remember that no matter how big or strong your feelings feel, they will eventually pass.

FEELINGS TIMELINE

Feelings growing . . .

Freaking out!

Calming down

THIS TOO SHALL PASS

There's an old folktale about a powerful king who told his advisor to find a ring that can make a happy person feel sad and a sad person feel happy. The advisor searched every jewelry store in the land, looking at rings with the finest diamonds and rubies money could buy, but he couldn't find the ring. One day, he was out walking in a poor neighborhood and came across an old woman selling a bunch of different antiques. The advisor asked if the woman had heard of this ring, and she showed him a tarnished silver ring with four words engraved on it: *This too shall pass*—a reminder that happy times won't last forever, but neither will sad ones. The king's advisor had found the ring.

• **Feelings are meant to be felt, not fixed.** It's soooo tempting to just want to make bad feelings go away. Nobody likes to feel sad or lonely or angry or confused or anxious. But just like cookies are meant to be eaten and Frisbees are meant to be thrown, feelings are meant to be felt and they can get pretty twitchy when nobody's paying attention to them. The more you ignore your feelings or try to fix them, the more power they send to your buttons, which makes your buttons even easier to push!

TRUTH BOMB

OK, here's a big, super important truth bomb: You can't control your thoughts or feelings. You can *influence* them, but you can't control them.

51

As you continue getting to know your own thoughts, feelings, and body sensations, it's important to remember that you can't force yourself to feel something you don't feel or to *not* feel something when you do. You can't make yourself think about something you've never even heard of, and you definitely can't make yourself *not* think about something that's on your mind. Sure, you can influence your feelings—for example, you probably feel happier when you get to watch a funny movie or play your favorite card game than when you have to scrub the toilet or get your braces tightened. And you have probably never thought about the Etruscan shrew (the world's tiniest mammal—it's super cute—look it up!) until now, when your thoughts were influenced by reading this book. So, yes, you can have an impact on what you think and feel, but you can't force yourself to feel or not feel a certain way or to think or not think specific thoughts. It's just the deal with human beings and our thoughts and feelings. We can't control them, and life is actually a whole lot easier when we can keep this in mind. Over the past couple of chapters, you've learned a lot about your brain, and your buttons, and your thoughts, feelings, and behaviors. Let's review it all in a quick quiz.

Your Brain, Buttons, Thoughts, Feelings, and Body Sensations

Imagine you just got home from a rough day at school and your parents tell you that they've invited your nemesis—the one kid you totally can't stand, the one who has been mean to you since second grade but never gets in trouble for it—to your birthday party since you invited all the other kids in your class.

1 You flip out before your parents can even finish their first sentence. Why was it so hard to stay calm?

A. Because it's a Monday and Mondays are the worst.

B. Because your dad is wearing his purple polka-dotted shirt and you can't stand that shirt.

C. Because your PFC is just too tired after a long, rough day at school and it just can't help keep you calm.

D. Because parents, duh.

❷ You're having a hard time listening to what your parents are saying. Is this because:

A. They're talking too fast.

B. You're thinking too hard and you can't listen to them at the same time.

C. This bad news pushed your buttons and triggered your limbic system (aka inner Safety Squirrel), which is so busy freaking out that you can't focus on the words coming out of your parents' mouths.

D. The minute your parents started talking, you put on your headphones and turned on your favorite song.

❸ You know your nemesis is going to ruin your party. Is this:

A. The truth.

B. A feeling.

C. A thought.

D. The topic of your next essay for English class.

❹ You're trying hard not to cry about this. Are your tears:

A. Nothing. Geez. Why are you even asking?

B. Allergies.

C. A body sensation that might be a clue that you might be feeling something, like anger, frustration, or being overwhelmed.

D. The result of all those onions you were cutting.

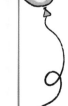

❺ You say each of the following things to your parents. Which one describes your feelings in the moment?

A. You care more about the other kid's feelings than mine!

B. I feel like you're trying to ruin my party!

C. I'm so mad right now!

D. Forget it. I don't even want a stupid party!

❻ You try to explain to your parents all the reasons why this kid absolutely cannot come to your party. Is this:

A. A feeling.

B. A whole bunch of thoughts that prove you are right and they are wrong.

C. A behavior.

D. Your one and only chance in the world at having a fun birthday.

Answer: The correct answer for each of these questions is C. You're getting good at understanding what pushes your buttons, why you flip out, and when you're thinking thoughts, feeling feelings, or experiencing something in your body. Didn't get them all right? That's OK! This stuff can take a little while to figure out, but it gets much easier with practice.

The Most Important Thing to Remember

Thoughts, feelings, and body sensations are the power behind your buttons. Freaking out is the behavior that happens when your buttons are pushed.

We'll talk more about buttons through the rest of the book, but coming up next is noticing what gives your buttons their power.

Chapter 5

LISTENING TO
YOUR BODY
AND YOUR BUTTONS

B y now you know that you have thoughts, feelings, and body sensations, and you're starting to get a sense of the differences between them. And you know that the stronger and more intense your thoughts, feelings, and body sensations are, the bigger, brighter, and more pushable your buttons become.

The next step is to get better at *noticing* when you're having a thought, feeling, or body sensation. This is important because when you realize that your buttons are super sensitive and pushable, you can do things to focus your thoughts, calm down your feelings, and take care of your buttons, all of which will **A)** make your buttons smaller, dimmer, and harder to push, and **B)** make it less likely that you'll freak out if and when those buttons are pushed anyway. Let me give you an example.

Imagine you're sitting in class, sort of doing your work but mostly drawing ninja hamsters shooting lasers. All of a sudden, your teacher looks at you and casually mentions that the principal wants to see you after class.

Maybe you've actually been sent to the principal once before. It was in third grade, for something you definitely didn't do but still got in trouble for and the whole thing was horrible and you never want it to happen again. So now you're desperately trying to figure out what you might have done wrong, but you can't remember doing anything wrong, so that means there must be something else wrong. (Hint: You're thinking. A lot.)

Your head starts throbbing and your shoulders get all tense and you're having a really hard time focusing on your drawing. (Hint: You've got a lot of sensations in your body.)

To top it all off, you're super anxious waiting for class to end but you're freaked out about class actually ending because you're pretty sure you don't want to hear whatever the principal has to say. (Hint: You're feeling lots of feelings right now!)

You've worked yourself into such a tizzy (meaning your buttons are huge and super pushable) that when you bump into your best friend on your way out of class and they ask you what's wrong, you snap at them to leave you alone already and you stomp off. By the time you get to the principal's office, you're so worked up that the principal has to repeat the news twice:

You've won the school-wide poetry contest.

Now, at this point you're probably wondering what exactly is the point of this whole story?

The point is to give you an example of how your thoughts and feelings make your buttons super-duper pushable.

Just to review: *Nothing bad happened.* All that happened was your teacher told you to check in with the principal and the principal told you that you won a writing contest. That's it. But your thoughts and feelings spun so far out of control and your buttons got so big and bright that all it took was one little question from your best friend to send you over the edge.

Now, the next time you're in a situation when you're thinking thoughts and feeling feelings (which is pretty much all the time), you have two choices:

FUN FREAK OUT FACT

Neuroscientists estimate that people think about 70,000 thoughts EVERY SINGLE DAY. That's a whole lotta power going to your buttons, and it doesn't even include your feelings and body sensations!

Option A) Do nothing, by which I mean, keep doing whatever it is you're doing. Most of the time, this will work out just fine.

Option B) Do something, by which I mean behave in a certain way that will calm those buttons down and make it less likely that you'll freak out.

Sometimes Option A works, but other times you really need Option B, which is what we're going to talk about now.

TRUTH BOMB

Just like you can't catch a ball if you don't realize it's coming at you, you can't choose what to do about your thoughts and feelings if you don't even realize you're having them. It's the *realizing* that gives you the power to decide what to do next.

When you take a second to listen to your body and notice what you're thinking and feeling, you're tapping into your PFC and giving yourself the best possible chance to make the best possible choice. But if you never listen or notice, then your limbic system (aka Safety Squirrel) will keep on running the show. And just like squirrels, your limbic system is wired to fight, flee, freeze, flip out, and fix—which is exactly what we're trying to avoid here.

So what do you need to notice and what do you do with what you notice? Your body, thoughts, and feelings are a great place to start.

HEAD, SHOULDERS, KNEES, AND TOES: CHECKING IN WITH YOUR BODY

Your body is directly connected to your buttons. When you've had enough sleep and enough to eat and nothing hurts and you don't need to pee, your buttons are likely to be nice and calm. But when you're exhausted and hungry and your knee is throbbing or your stomach is grumbling and you really gotta go to the bathroom, your buttons will be begging to be pushed!

Sometimes we know what's happening in our bodies, but lots of times we don't. And when we don't realize how sore or stiff or stuffed up we are, we can't choose to take care of our bodies (and our buttons).

The trick is to check in with your body. If there's something going on that's lighting up your buttons, taking care of it might be just what you need to avoid a freak out!

First, try asking yourself the following questions:

❶ Am I **hungry or thirsty**? When was the last time I ate or drank something?

❷ Am I **tired**? Did I sleep well last night? Have I had an exhausting day?

❸ Do I need to go to the **bathroom**?

❹ Am I in **pain**, **sore**, **or uncomfortable** anywhere in my body?

If you're hungry, can you get a snack? If you're tired, can you take a nap or make a plan to go to sleep early? If you need to go to the bathroom, well, um, you should do that. And if you're in pain, is there anything you can do to feel better? Do you need to talk to an adult about it?

You can also check in with your body by practicing C.A.L.M., which stands for Chest, Arms, Legs, and Mouth.

First, check in with your **chest**. How does it feel? Tight? Relaxed? Does it feel like there's something heavy on it, or does it feel open and calm? And how about your breathing? Are you holding your breath? Or breathing too fast or hard?

Next, notice what's going on with your **arms**. Are you clenching your fists? Are your shoulders tense and tight and up by your ears? If so, drop your shoulders, spread your fingers, and shake it all out.

From there, focus on your **legs**. Are your thighs or calf muscles especially tight? You might give yourself a little massage, shake out your legs, or wiggle your toes. And if you can't stop tapping your toes or bouncing your feet, it might be a sign that your body wants to move more. If this is the case, can you run around the block, shoot some hoops, or turn on your favorite tunes and have a little dance party?

Finally, it's time to check in with your **mouth**. Are you tensing your jaw? Grinding your teeth? Chewing your tongue? If you notice any of these, try to relax your mouth, let your jaw drop a little bit, and loosen your tongue.

Asking yourself those questions and practicing C.A.L.M. can help relax your body, power down your buttons, and help you feel less stressed.

The next step is to notice your thoughts.

WHAT ARE YOU THINKING?

Generally speaking, there are three kinds of thoughts.

Helpful thoughts are ones that help us feel clearer, calmer, more confident, less stressed, and less confused. These thoughts will help your buttons get and stay smaller, dimmer, and less pushable. Here are a few examples:

- I can do this.
- Everything is going to be OK.
- I have a lot of options and choices.
- I can get the help I need.
- I'm grateful for what I have.
- My friends and family love me and support me.
- I can handle this.
- It's OK to make mistakes.

- Everything is OK (or it will be).
- This hard situation will pass.
- I'm not failing; I'm just learning ways that don't work.
- I have lots of strategies for handling this situation.
- I don't have to be perfect to be successful.
- I don't have to be perfect. Nobody is.
- Taco Cat spelled backward is Taco Cat.

Neutral thoughts aren't good or bad, and they're not necessarily connected to any of your buttons. That means that while they might not calm down your buttons, they won't power them up either.

- My shirt is gray.
- My birthday is in June.
- I remembered my backpack.
- Tomorrow is Tuesday.
- My cat's name is Purrito.

Problematic thoughts are most likely to light up your buttons. Whether or not these thoughts are true, they're unhelpful because they're likely to make you feel angry, worried, confused, or overwhelmed.

- I'm not smart / strong / attractive / good enough.
- No one will believe me.

- Something bad will happen.
- My life will be ruined.
- It's going to hurt.
- It's never going to get better.
- No one likes me.
- I'm going to mess it up.
- I already totally messed it up.
- No one will ever forget what I did.
- No one will ever forgive me.
- I can't handle this situation.
- I'm the only one who _____.
- They won't understand.
- Everyone is judging me.
- I'll never be good at _____.
- I can't do this.
- I don't belong here.
- It won't be OK.
- I'll never ever get a cat.

One more thought about your thoughts: the same thought can be helpful, neutral, or problematic depending on where you are and what you're doing. Let's take the thought: "I'm ready to sleep."

If it's nighttime and you're super cozy in your bed, then thinking about how you're ready to go to sleep is either helpful or neutral. But if you're in the middle of class and your teacher just announced a pop quiz and you have a big softball game after school, thinking about sleep might stress you out, making it a problematic thought that could send more power to your buttons.

THE POWER OF W.A.I.T.ing

Sometimes you can have thoughts that happen so fast, you don't even realize you thought them—but they can still power up your buttons even if you have no idea it's happening! A great way to figure out what you're thinking is to stop whatever you're doing and W.A.I.T., which stands for **W**hat **A**m **I** **T**hinking?

W.A.I.T. is a simple question, but it's a super useful one because it helps you slow down long enough to notice your thoughts instead of getting all caught up in them. Maybe you'll notice that you're having helpful or neutral thoughts, and that's great. Carry on!

But if the thoughts you notice are problematic, you have a few other choices:

1 Remember that just because you think something, that doesn't make it true or real or accurate. You don't have to believe everything you think!

2 Give your brain something else to think about. Count to ten or count to twenty-one by threes. Turn on your favorite song. Reread your favorite graphic novel. Recite a prayer or phrase that calms you down. Talk to a friend. Focus on a crafts project or recipe or sport.

3 Check in with your feelings.

TRUTH BOMB

The next time you W.A.I.T. you might be tempted to ask yourself *Why Am I Thinking,* or *Why Am I Thinking This Thing That I Am Thinking?* Try not to worry about the *why.* Sometimes we might be able to figure it out, but it's also possible we'll never know why a specific memory or idea popped into our brains. Tap into your PFC and focus on the *what* so you can keep calming down.

NAME IT TO TAME IT:
FIGURE OUT WHAT YOU'RE FEELING

We've talked about noticing your body sensations and thoughts. Now it's time to dig into your feelings.

Strong, intense, or unpleasant feelings power up your buttons faster than just about anything else. And yucky feelings feel, well, yucky, so you may try to ignore them or avoid them. Unfortunately, that doesn't usually work. Feelings want to be felt, not ignored. When you don't feel them, they don't go away. They just hang out in your body and mess with your thoughts, powering up your buttons until someone pushes them and you freak out.

Totally not what we're going for here.

Fortunately, there's a really useful strategy for managing big feelings: *naming them.*

There's something magical about **A)** acknowledging that you're having a feeling, and **B)** finding the right word to describe it. You've probably had this experience before. Think back to a time when you were upset about something and you talked to someone who really listened. And then they said something about you or your feelings that was exactly right. The minute they said it, you felt completely understood and maybe even a little less confused. You might

have cried or even felt a tiny bit worse at first, but as this person kept listening and talking, you felt calmer and better.

Sometimes we need someone else to help us figure out what we're feeling, but it's also something we can do for ourselves each time we notice and name what we're feeling. It's like once you give them a name, your feelings go, "Whew! You finally realized I'm here! Thank goodness! Now I can stop nagging you quite so hard." And as your feelings calm down, your buttons do, too. There's even a handy little rhyme to help you remember this: **name it to tame it**.

As simple as this seems (and it is), it's not always so easy to do, for a few different reasons:

1 **Bad feelings feel bad.** And most folks don't like feeling bad, so it can be hard to make yourself slow down and notice what you're feeling because you want that feeling to be over and gone fast. (Remember: Just because something *feels* bad, that doesn't mean it's wrong. Also, feelings don't last forever! Most feelings only last a few minutes, but even if they stick around a little longer, they will pass.)

2 When we're overwhelmed by big feelings, **our limbic systems** are in charge. And remember, that Safety Squirrel doesn't care about slowing down and naming things. It's just trying to figure out how to keep you safe, which often ends up looking like a freak out.

❸ **Feelings can be confusing and hard to name,** especially if we're feeling lots of big feelings all at once. For example, if you're headed off to sleepaway camp for the first time, you might feel excited, anxious, eager, and sad all at once. Feeling all those feelings at the same time can be really confusing!

The good news is that the more we practice naming our feelings, the easier it gets! A great way to practice naming your feelings is to have a list to pick from. In fact, just reading a list like this will help power up your PFC and calm down your Safety Squirrel. Here is a list to help you get started:

Afraid – Amazed – Angry – Annoyed

Anxious – Bored – Brave – Cheated

Confused – Cranky – Disappointed

Disgusted – Eager – Embarrassed

Excited – Frustrated – Grouchy – Happy

Hopeless – Impatient – Insulted

Intrigued – Jealous – Lonely – Mad

Nervous – Offended – Overwhelmed

Panicked – Playful – Proud – Relieved

Sad – Shocked – Stressed – Stuck

Surprised – Terrified – Tired – Trapped

Uncomfortable – Upset – Worried

QUICK QUIZ

The most effective way to control your thoughts and feelings is:

A. Notice that you're having a thought or feeling something.

B. Write out a list of all the thoughts and feelings you're having.

C. Unclench your fists and take three deep breaths.

D. Figure out where your feelings are showing up in your body.

E. None of the above.

Answer: E. None of the above. Remember—you can't control how you're feeling and what you're thinking. What you can do is notice what's going on in your body, mind, and with your emotions, and make choices that will help you feel better, think more clearly, and make your buttons harder to push.

The Most Important Thing to Remember

You can't control your thoughts and feelings, but you can influence and *notice* them. Noticing gives you options.

There's one more thing you can do to maintain calm, too: figure out what pushes your buttons, and what to do about those button pushers. And that's what we're going to talk about next.

Chapter 6

WHERE THERE'S
A BUTTON,
THERE'S A PUSHER

So far we've talked about your buttons (the invisible connection between you and whatever is happening in your life) and what powers them up (your body sensations, thoughts, and feelings). But here's the thing—*buttons don't do anything if they're never pushed.* Think about all of the devices and machines in your life that have buttons: phones, computers, microwaves, dishwashers, washers, dryers, etc. Even if they're connected to a source of power, they never turn on or light up or do anything at all unless their buttons are pushed.

We humans are the same way. If nothing ever pushed our buttons, we'd never freak out. But there will always be people, situations, and experiences that push your buttons. You'll never be able to avoid them completely, no matter how hard you try. Fortunately, you can get better at dealing with the button pushers in your life by 1) figuring out who and what they are, and 2) avoiding them whenever you can.

Let's start with step 1: figuring out who and what pushes your buttons. As you read the following examples, try to imagine whether a similar situation might push your buttons.

EXAMPLE #1: TERRIBLE TUESDAY

It's a Tuesday and you've been tired all day. It's raining, you got tomato sauce all over your new shirt, you had a pop quiz that you totally weren't ready for and almost certainly bombed, and the annoying kid on the bus wouldn't stop bragging about his new video game, the one you really want but your parents refuse to buy.

You finally get home, head up to your room, and pop on your headphones. Just as you're starting to relax with

your favorite music, your mom calls out from down the hall. She reminds you that you need to clean out your lunch box, study for your science quiz, and take a shower before dinner. Before you even realize what's happening, you burst into tears. It's just too much. You can't handle it.

Even though your mom wasn't being rude, mean, or saying anything surprising or confusing, your buttons were so sensitive that her reminders pushed them instantly.

EXAMPLE #2: WHINY WINNIE

You're at summer camp, one of your favorite places on earth. You love swimming, softball, scavenger hunts, and sneaking out of the cabin with your counselor to get ice cream from the mess hall after lights out. You're having a great time, except there's one person who just makes you cringe. Winnie. She's the new girl who is constantly complaining about everything. You know you should probably ignore her, but she just won't stop and it's so hard to tune her out! The more she whines and complains, the more annoyed you get, and you wish she would just go away. Finally, as you're all walking to the campfire at the end of the day, Winnie says something mean about your favorite counselor.

You can't handle it. That final comment makes you explode. You whirl around, get right up in Winnie's face, and yell at her that if she hates camp so much, why doesn't she just go home! In this case, Winnie's whining pushed all of your buttons.

EXAMPLE #3: ACCIDENTAL ACCIDENT

You're out running errands with your grandma. It's been a pretty good day, and you're both in good moods. You're in the car, stopped at a stoplight, when suddenly you hear a loud crashing sound just as the car jerks forward. Your grandma shrieks, you feel your heart start racing, and before you can figure out what happened, you burst into tears, start screaming, and

you can't calm down. Even though you and your grandma are fine, the sudden rear-ending pushed your buttons hard and fast enough to send you from Totally Fine to Totally Freaking Out in just a few seconds.

LOTS OF THINGS CAN PUSH YOUR BUTTONS

Unexpected, unwanted, unpleasant, and unsafe people, situations, and experiences are all potential button pushers. That doesn't mean every one will definitely push your buttons. It just means they *could*.

Button pushers can include people, situations, and experiences that:

A Have absolutely nothing to do with you but push your buttons anyway, like an ambulance siren wailing in your ear, or the rain that ruined recess.

B Aren't directed at you specifically, but are in your life and impact you, like when your best friend in the whole world moves across the country or your field hockey team gets a new coach who makes you do the worst running drills ever.

C Are absolutely about you, like when your nemesis at school purposely shared your crummy test score with the entire class or your twin sister told your parents that you were the one who spilled maple syrup down the heater vent, which is why the whole house smells like pancakes every time the heat comes on.

Other button pushers might include losing your lucky baseball hat, hearing something scary on the news, a science class that somehow manages to be both boring and confusing at the same time, your favorite coach breaking her leg and missing practice for the rest of the season, or your parents fighting in their bedroom, where they think you can't hear them but you definitely can.

Sometimes that scary news or science class might go right over your head and not get anywhere near your buttons at all. Or they could just be another

FUN FREAK OUT FACT Have you ever had a terrible, horrible, no good, very bad day? If so, you're not alone! There's even a classic picture book (which was made into a TV show and a movie) about those bad days. *Alexander and the Terrible, Horrible, No Good, Very Bad Day* was written by Judith Viorst, who based the story of Alexander and his brothers Anthony and Nick on her experience with her own three sons.

jab at your buttons that gives you lots of thoughts and feelings but you're able to stay calm. Or they might be the very thing that sends you over the edge into a full-on freak out.

It all depends on how sensitive your buttons already are in that moment, and how hard and fast they're pushed.

A LONGER LIST OF PEOPLE, SITUATIONS, AND EXPERIENCES THAT MIGHT PUSH YOUR BUTTONS

As you read this list, try to notice if these are experiences or situations that push your buttons or not. You might even think of button pushers that aren't on this list! Either way, there's no right or wrong answer. It's just about getting to know yourself and what is most likely to send you into fight, flight, freeze, flip out, or fix.

- Running late to, or missing, something important
- Being lied to
- Being interrupted
- Realizing your friends are hanging out without you
- Being ignored

- A stressful or important test, presentation, game, or competition
- Being sick or injured
- Watching someone you know get sick or injured
- Failing a test or losing a game
- Unfair situations
- Your sibling saying or doing just about anything
- People taking or using your things without asking
- Having something stolen from you
- Losing or breaking things you care about
- Getting bad news
- People bumping up against you or touching you when you don't want to be touched
- Loud, unexpected noises
- Not understanding what to do
- Being bossed around or told what to do
- Having too much to do
- Not having enough to do
- Having to meet new people or try new things

As you think about the people and experiences that push your buttons, here are a few things to remember:

• **Some button pushers are universal—they push almost everyone's buttons.** These include people, experiences, and situations that leave you feeling unsafe, powerless, disrespected, or like you're being treated unfairly. Someone leaping out from a dark corner. Having to spend the afternoon with the mean neighbor. Having your things stolen from your locker. Being ignored by kids you thought were your friends. Push push push.

• **Other button pushers are unique, or specific to just some people.** The sound of someone chewing might drive you completely bananapants, while your BFF doesn't even notice. The way Great Uncle Edwin comments on your shoes every time he sees you might push hard on your buttons but not your brother's. Some people love a good storm, but thunder and lightning might totally freak you out. Push push pushity push.

• **The things that push your buttons will change over time.** When you were a toddler you might have had a full-on tantrum over whether your toast was cut in a rectangle or a triangle or a heart. Hopefully, you're a little more flexible about your toast by now, but you have no patience for kids who cheat at capture the flag. Don't worry, chances are good that capture the flag won't push your buttons quite so much—if at all—in a few years.

• **Something that pushes your buttons today might not bother you at all tomorrow.** It all depends on what else is going on for you, how you're feeling, what you're thinking, how your body is doing, and how sensitive your buttons are at the moment.

• **You might have some control over some button pushers in your life, but not most of them.** If you know a certain kid at school drives you absolutely nuts, you can ask your teacher not to pair you with them for class projects. But there may not be a lot you can do about getting your teeth cleaned or having to spend Thanksgiving dinner listening to your cousin brag about winning the state cheerleading championship. Take space from your button pushers when you can, but remember this: There will always be things that push your buttons, and it's not because you've done anything wrong. It's just because you're a human being living a life.

Your Buttons and What Pushes Them

The more you know about your buttons and how they work, the less surprised you'll be when someone or something pushes them and the more control you'll have over how you respond. And that's what this quiz is all about—your tendencies and what you are most likely to do in a given situation. There are no right or wrong answers. Just pick the answer that feels like the best match for you!

1 You're having a rough day at school. You keep having to ask for the hall pass so no one will see you cry. Is it most likely because:

A. You didn't sleep well the night before because your brother has a cold and his cough kept waking you up.

B. You found out that the new kid in your class asked your two closest friends to go skating, but you weren't invited.

C. You got in a huge fight with your parents that morning because they wouldn't let you wear your new ripped jeans to school.

D. You have to go to the eye doctor this afternoon and you hate the drops they always put in your eyes. You can't stop thinking about it.

2 You just exploded at your brother—you screamed, threw a pencil, and slammed the door in his face. What's the most likely cause?

A. He didn't actually do anything so bad, but you've got a sore tooth and it hurts so badly that simply seeing him irritates you.

B. All of your friends got the arts elective and you got stuck in the current affairs elective without a single person you actually like.

C. The minute you got home from school, your brother started telling you to empty your lunch box and do your chores. Who does he think he is?

D. He refused to practice basketball with you and now there's no way you'll make the team.

❸ You have to go to math tutoring every Thursday afternoon and you can't stand it. Every time you look at a page of equations, your brain freezes up and you have no idea what's going on. Is it because:

A. By the time you get there after school you're starving and you never remember to bring a snack.

B. Most of your friends are in karate but you can't go because it's at the same time as tutoring.

C. Your tutor is constantly snapping at you to pay attention and focus and write more neatly.

D. You're too distracted by what might happen if you can't bring your math grade up.

4 Now that you're at a new middle school, you have to walk to and from the bus stop on your own. You've begged and promised to do your homework, clean your room, walk the dog, and set the table without being asked if only your parents will drive you. Is it because:

A. The loud noise of the traffic on your walk home is the worst sound ever!

B. Your parents drove your older siblings but they're not driving you because they're both working full-time now.

C. The walk home alone is so boring and your parents insist you walk straight home every afternoon without stopping at the ice cream store, the bookstore, or anywhere fun.

D. You're scared of the barking dogs along the way even though they're behind fences.

Answers:

If you got mostly A's: Your thoughts, feelings, and body sensations can make your buttons so bright and sensitive that almost anything will push them. It's just how you're wired!

If you got mostly B's: Feeling rejected, ignored, or excluded really pushes your buttons.

If you got mostly C's: Being bossed around and controlled is a major button pusher for you.

If you got mostly D's: Anxiety and/or fear send so much power to your buttons and make them so bright, sensitive, and pushable that everything pushes them.

If you got a bunch of different answers: That's OK! We all have different thoughts and feelings that light up our buttons, and a lot of different people, situations, and experiences push them. Now that you know you have buttons, you'll become more aware of them and get to know them better and better.

Now that you're figuring out who and what pushes your buttons, you're ready for step 2—figuring out how to avoid the people and situations that push your buttons as often as you can. The good news is that you can avoid some of them, some of the time.

Let's go back to the examples from the beginning of this chapter.

In the Terrible Tuesday example, it was your mother's requests that pushed your buttons. You can't avoid your mother, cleaning out your lunch box, or showering, but maybe you can ask your mom to leave you a reminder note instead of yelling down the hall, or give you a little downtime before you have to do everything.

DON'T FORGET
To CLEAN OUT YOUR LUNCHBOX!
HOPE YOU HAD A GOOD DAY!
LOVE MOM

TRUTH BOMB

Families do a lot of button pushing, mostly because they spend so much time together. You push your parents' buttons and they push yours. Brothers and sisters push one another's buttons all day long. Siblings can get into fights as often as eight times an hour. That's about once every seven minutes. That's a whole lotta button pushing and freaking out!

In the Whiny Winnie story, the most effective way to avoid Winnie would be to take space from her whenever you can. Maybe you walk to the lake with some friends or sit at the opposite end of the table from her. And if it all gets to be too much, you can talk with the counselor or another trusted adult to get some support and advice about what else you can do.

Lastly, there's the Accidental Accident. Sadly, this is one of those situations where there is nothing you or your grandma could have done. Unfortunately, these things happen and we can't stop them. The best thing you can do in these situations is to notice that your buttons have been pushed, try not to blame yourself for freaking out, and do whatever you can to get calm and take care of yourself afterward.

The Most Important Thing to Remember

There will always be people, situations, and experiences that push your buttons. It doesn't feel great, but it doesn't mean you're doing anything wrong! It's just part of life. The trick is to recognize that your buttons have been pushed and do whatever you can to calm your feelings, focus your thoughts, and take care of your body.

Knowing what pushes your buttons and avoiding your button pushers as often as possible are the first two steps toward not freaking out. Sadly, it's just not possible to avoid every single button pusher, so it's really helpful to know how to keep your buttons as calm as possible as often as possible, and how to calm down and feel better after your buttons have been pushed and you've freaked out anyway. And that's what we're going to talk about in the next two chapters.

Chapter 7

HOW TO MAKE
YOUR BUTTONS
HARDER TO PUSH

Now that you know what powers *up* your buttons, what makes them bigger, brighter, and easier to push, and what pushes them, it's time to talk about how to power them *down*. There are things you can do that will make your buttons smaller, dimmer, and way more push-proof. The less pushable your buttons are, the less likely you'll be to freak out when you need to deal with unexpected, unwanted, and unpleasant people, situations, and experiences.

The secret is in your BuRPs.

And no, I'm not talking about the sound that blasts out of your mouth in the middle of dinner and earns you a stern look. I'm talking about your **Bu**tton **R**eduction **P**ractices, which are behaviors you can do that will calm your buttons down. These include strategies that you can use every day, like getting outside, listening to your favorite song, or taking a long drink of water. BuRPS make your buttons harder to push by helping you focus your thoughts, feel your feelings, and take care of your body. (And even though you may not realize it, they also calm down your limbic system / Safety Squirrel and help put your PFC back in charge.) But that's not all—lots of BuRPs are really fun, and doing something fun is a great way to feel better!

> **FUN FREAK OUT FACT** The more you burp, the less you fart. It's all about releasing the gas that's built up in your body, one way or another. (Also, the more you practice your BuRPs, the less likely you are to react with F.A.R.T.y outbursts!)

THE ABC's OF BURPs

Imagine if your first-grade teacher tried to teach you how to read by starting with words like "receipt," "asthma," "questionnaire," and "subtle." My guess is that wouldn't have gone very well, which is why your teacher started with the ABC's and short, simple words like "car," "dog," and "hat." Simple is the best way to learn something new, including your BuRPs. And that's why we're going to start with the ABC's of BuRPing.

As you read through the list below of twenty-six BuRPs, try to notice which ones might be a good match for you. Maybe you're already doing some of them, or maybe there are some you've never tried before but are curious about.

This isn't a complete list of BuRPs. Not even close! You can make up your own BuRPs if you'd like—anything that clears your thinking, calms your feelings, and takes care of your body is a great choice.

A — ALWAYS AN OPTION. It doesn't matter if you're in the middle of class, practice, or starring in your leading role on stage, BuRPing is *always* an option. Don't believe me? Check out BuRP B!

B — BREATHE. If you could pick only one BuRP, pick this one. Every time you take a slow breath, a deep breath, or just remember to breathe at all, it's like sending a text message directly to your nervous system saying, "It's OK.

Everything is OK. No need to freak out or even think about freaking out."

Any time you think of it, just take a couple of deep breaths or count your breaths or, you know, just breathe. (Just don't swallow your breath unless you actually want to burp for real.)

C — CUT YOURSELF A WHOLE LOTTA SLACK. Whenever you notice that you're judging yourself or feeling bad about your mistakes, try to remember that 1) no one is perfect, 2) you don't have to be perfect to be awesome, and 3) figuring out how to stay calm when things are chaotic is hard for everyone. Try talking to yourself the way a good friend would talk to you.

D — DRINK SOMETHING, preferably water. Dehydration (not having enough water in your body) can make you tired and cranky, so grab your water bottle and take a big sip as often as possible.

FUN FREAK OUT FACT

A newborn baby's body is about 78 percent water, and adult bodies are about 55 percent water, which means you're probably around 67 percent water. The water in your body helps regulate your temperature, bring nutrients to your cells, and—coolest of all—it's like a shock absorber for your brain and spinal cord. So drink up, dude!

E — EAT A SNACK. The next time you're feeling tired, sad, or mad, try to remember the last time you ate something. Your feelings might be a legitimate response to whatever's going on in your life, but it might also be that you're hungry. Or, shall I say, hangry (hungry + angry)?

I'm not saying you should head for the fridge every time you feel angry or anxious or bored or confused. If hunger isn't the actual issue, then eating won't calm your buttons down. But hanger is real, which is why grabbing an apple can be a great choice.

F — FRIENDS AND/OR FAMILY. Spending time with people you care about and who care about you is one of your most powerful BuRPs. Whether you're feeling amazing, horrible, or anything in between, knowing you're not alone is a great way to keep your buttons nice and calm. (Hot tip: In person is best, but when that's not an option, virtual works, too!)

G — GRIN AND GIGGLE. Or giggle and grin. Or grin but don't giggle. Or, hardest of all—giggle without grinning. Doing something—anything—every day that makes you smile and laugh is an awesome BuRP. Here's a joke to get you started:

Why don't pirates take a shower before they walk the plank? They just wash up onshore!

H — GET A HOBBY. Organize your bobbleheads. Go on a bird-watching walk. Toss a Frisbee. Strum your ukulele. Practice photography. Make a scrapbook. Put together a puzzle. Sew a cape for your cat. Fold an origami crane. Shoot hoops. Learn a card trick. Solve a crossword. Make your grandmother's famous chocolate-chip banana bread. Practice hacky sacking. It doesn't matter what the hobby is as long as it's something you like doing that lowers your stress.

I — BE IDLE. Sometimes your brain and your body just need a break. You need to be idle, as in space out and do nothing. Lie in the grass and stare at the clouds. Sit on a bench on the playground and watch the squirrels run around. Spread out on your bed and daydream. Let your thoughts wander. Maybe you'll have a deep thought or realization, or maybe you'll think nothing at all. Either way, it can be a great BuRP.

J — JOURNAL. Sometimes your hands are better at figuring things out than your brain or heart is. So grab your tablet and stylus or a fancy journal and your favorite pen or the back of your math test and a pencil you found on the floor. Write, doodle, or draw—whatever you prefer! You can keep it all forever, delete it, or tear it up into a million pieces as soon as it's done. Also, writing, drawing, or doodling can be a hobby *and* a way to be creative, so bonus BuRP points for you!

K — KICK A BALL. Or throw it, bounce it, or hit it with a racket or a bat. Do it on your own or with someone else. There's just something about a ball that makes for an awesome BuRP. (Just take it outside or you might find yourself on the receiving end of a very big parental freak out.)

If you're stuck inside on a rainy day, try marbles. They're not just beautiful little glass balls that come in a ton of cool colors and designs and are fun to collect. There are a lots of different marble games you can play on your own or with a sibling or friend!

L — LISTEN TO WHATEVER YOU NEED TO LISTEN TO. Looking for a boost of energy? Try rocking out to "Happy" by Pharrell Williams or "Stayin' Alive" by the Bee Gees. Feeling down and need a good cry? "Everybody Hurts" by R.E.M. or "When the Party's Over" by Billie Eilish are great choices. Oh, and if you need to get your anger out, a rage anthem (yep, that's a thing!) is always a good choice. Not feeling the music vibe at all? Your favorite audiobook or podcast might just hit the spot.

M — MOVE YOUR BODY. I know you already know this, but it's so important that I'm going to say it again: Your feelings live in your body, and moving your body helps your feelings move, loosen up, and lighten up. Also, if your attention is focused on moving your body, you're way less likely to be all caught up in your thoughts. So go for a walk, grab a Hula-Hoop, hop on your bike, jump in the pool, run up and down the stairs or around the block, do some jumping jacks, or go

back to that awesome song you were just listening to and get your groove on.

N — NOTICE. Noticing is the difference between just doing something without thinking and realizing what you're doing and knowing that you're doing it. You can notice your thoughts, feelings, and behaviors, and you can also notice anything you can see, hear, touch, smell, or taste. Noticing is a powerful BuRP for three reasons:

1 It helps calm down your feelings by engaging your PFC. Your PFC isn't just about planning, figuring out, and calming down, it's also the noticing center of your brain. Even if what you're noticing has nothing to do with what you're feeling, it still works because it's still powering up your PFC!

❷ Noticing focuses your thinking. When you notice something in the here and now, even if it's the color of your sneakers, your thoughts won't be spiraling through worries about the futures or regrets about the past.

❸ Noticing gets you out of the storm of your own thoughts and feelings so you can clearly see what's going on around you instead of making assumptions or jumping to conclusions that might not be true or helpful.

O – GET OUTSIDE. There's something magical about going outside. Put on your headphones, or grab your journal, soccer ball, or camera, and head on out. And if you can't get outside because it's raining like crazy or you're on an eight-hour car ride to Grandma's house, can you open the window for some fresh air? Or at least look out the window for a few minutes? Every little bit helps!

P — PRAY. Or chant. Or recite your favorite mantra, poem, or the lyrics to a song that you really love. Repeating words that are meaningful to you will help you clear your mind, focus your thoughts, and calm your feelings.

Q — QUACK LIKE A DUCK. Sometimes you just need to yell. And if you're in a place where you can yell without making a scene, starting a fight, freaking anyone out, or getting in trouble, then totally do that. But if that's not an option, try quacking like a duck, clucking like a chicken, or making some other ridiculous noise—it will have the same effect. It sounds bonkers, I know, but don't knock it 'til you've tried it.

R — READ SOMETHING that distracts you, cracks you up, makes you feel something, or inspires you. Your favorite magazine or catalogue. A graphic novel about a superhero who only wears underwear and fights evil toilets. A collection of poems your great uncle wrote. A novel that makes you sob, but in a good way that somehow leaves you feeling oddly better when you're done. Heck, you might even reach for that book your parents suggested—the one that actually turned out to be good even though you'll never ever admit it to them.

S — SNUGGLE. Whether it's a parent, a stuffed animal, or your cat or dog, snuggles and hugs are powerful ways to calm down and feel safe and connected.

T — THANK YOU. You can say thank you to your teacher for letting you retake the math test. You can thank your parents for  buying your favorite crackers, thank your pet hamster for being so darn cute, or thank the sun for shining on the day of your big game. You can thank me for writing this amazing book or thank your sprained finger for healing in time for your cello recital. It doesn't really matter who or what you thank; just taking the time to notice something deserving of your gratitude and appreciation is a great way to BuRP.

U — UNPLUG. Whether you're texting with your friends, playing your favorite game, or scrolling through cat videos on your cousin's Instagram account, screen time is very likely to make you cranky. It's not your fault or your friend's fault and it's definitely not those cute cats' fault. It's just what too much screen time does. You don't have to give up screens forever; just long enough to give your brain and body a break from those apps, games, and shows every day.

V — VOLUNTEER TO HELP SOMEONE. Remember the last time you did something nice for someone? Maybe you

reviewed multiplication tables with your sister
or invited the new kid to join your after-
school art club or helped your teacher
stack all the chairs on the
desks. Or maybe you work
at a local soup kitchen or
animal shelter every month.
However you helped, it
probably felt pretty good or, at
the very least, got you out of
your own head long enough to
calm your buttons down.

W — GO FOR A WALK. So many possible BuRPs wrapped up
in just one walk. Right off the bat you're moving your body,
getting outside, and unplugging. But you can also notice
your breathing while you walk, or let your mind go idle as
you wonder and daydream or think about everything you
have to be thankful for. Or you can walk to the ice cream
shop with your sibling, neighbor, or best friend.

X — TAKE AN X-RAY OF YOUR BODY. I'm not talking about
an actual X-ray, just a quick internal X-ray. You can use the
C.A.L.M. technique, or start with your head and do a quick
scan of your body down to your toes. You can take a few
deep breaths, shake out your arms and legs, and give your

brain a break, or you can just take your X-ray and get back to whatever you're doing. Either way, it's a great way to bring your buttons down a notch.

Y — DO A LITTLE YOGA. Whether downward dog is your jam, or you'd rather hang out in happy baby, stretching out your body is an amazing way to clear your mind, relax your muscles, and release your stress. You can follow a yoga video or book or just stretch out your body in any way that feels good. It's not about whether you can touch your toes or bend all the way back, it's just about doing what feels good for your body and your breathing—bonus BuRP!

Z — GET YOUR ZZZZZZ'S! Sleep might be one of the best BuRPs in the history of BuRPs. Sleep isn't just necessary for growth, healing, and other body functions—it's also one of the best ways to turn down the power to your buttons and make them way less pushable. Sometimes when everything feels overwhelming, it might just be that your brain and your body are completely exhausted. A long night of sleep or a nap can be the reset you need.

Now that you've read the whole list, here are a few more reminders:

• **The more you BuRP, the less pushable your buttons will be.** Easy as that.

• **BuRPing works. Reading about BuRPs? Not so much.** You gotta actually run around the block, quack like a duck, or stretch out on the floor in order to calm down your buttons. Sitting on your bed and thinking about your BuRPs isn't going to release your pressure in the same way.

• **You don't have to do every BuRP.** Pick the ones you like or make up new ones if you want to. As long as whatever you're doing helps focus your thoughts, calm your feelings, and/or take care of your body, then it's a great BuRP.

• **Do the best you can with what you have.** If you're in class, a house of worship, practice, or another situation where you can't turn on your favorite song, can you sing it silently to yourself? If you're stuck in the back seat of the car where you can't do the jumping jacks that help you work your stress out, can you squeeze and relax your fists or raise and lower your shoulders?

• **Your BuRPs are practices,** which means they might seem weird or confusing at first, but the more you actually do them, the easier and more natural they'll become. Hang in there. You got this.

• **Don't wait to practice BuRPing.** It can be super tempting to ignore your BuRPs until you really need them—meaning when you're stressed out or about to freak out. But it's really hard to learn and do new things when you're overwhelmed. The more you practice your BuRPs when you're feeling calm and thinking clearly, the easier it will be to BuRP when you're on the verge of freaking out!

• **The more stressful things are, the more you need to BuRP.** When the pressure is really on, BuRPs will help you stay calm and not freak out.

• Finally, **you're in charge of your BuRPs.** You decide if and when to practice them, and you decide if you want to BuRP the same way every time, or if you want to switch it up.

BUT WHAT IF YOUR BURPS AREN'T ENOUGH?

Sometimes, BuRPs aren't enough. Sometimes, no matter how often or how well you sleep, stay hydrated, move your body, and snuggle Fido, your buttons are still big, bright, and pushable and even the tiniest touch sends you into fight, flight, freeze, flip out, or fix mode.

That happens to lots of folks. And when it does, you're gonna need a new plan, maybe one with some advanced BuRPs, like taking a mental health day or talking to a trusted adult.

Your first option is a **mental health day**. It used to be that kids could only get out of school and adults could only get out of work if they were sick, like with a bad cold or the flu. But now there's another option—a mental health day. This is when you take a day off because you've been dealing with too much stress or pressure and you just need a break. This is a totally legit thing to do, *but only if you take them seriously,* by which I mean:

A Don't ask for a mental health day if you don't need one. Mental health days aren't for avoiding tests you don't want to take or best friends you're mad at and don't want to see. If you try to use them too often, your parents won't believe you anymore!

B Use your mental health days wisely. Don't spend them doing things that light up your buttons, like spacing out in front of a screen, thinking about everything that's terrible about your life, or plotting revenge against your ex–best friend. Instead, go back to your BuRPs. Reread your favorite book, work on the comic book you've been drawing, go for a walk, do some gentle stretching, shoot some hoops, listen to the playlist you love, work on an art project, write in your journal, or even take a nap!

TRUTH BOMB

Kids rarely want to nap. Maybe it's because you still remember when your parents made you nap when you didn't want to. Or maybe it's because you're worried about missing out on something fun. But naps can be great BuRPs, so if you're worn out, give it a shot. Scientists have found that even a twenty-minute power nap can help improve your memory and mood and help you solve problems faster!

C Use your day off to think about what you need or changes you could make. Do you need some extra help in your classes? Or do you need to take a break from one of your extracurricular activities? Do you need help remembering to put down your phone earlier so you can get more sleep? Maybe you need to talk to an adult you trust, which brings us to your next advanced BuRP.

Your second option is **checking in with a trusted adult**, like a family member, coach, or teacher. Tell them what's going on. They might have some good advice or ideas for you, and even if they don't, sometimes just saying things out loud to someone who cares about you can help you feel better.

Another trusted adult you can talk to is a mental health therapist or counselor. If you're not sure exactly what a therapist does, you're not alone. Lots of kids and adults are confused about it, too. Therapists are kind of like a cross between a detective who helps you solve the mystery of what's going on with your thoughts, feelings, and behaviors, and a tour guide who will lead you through confusing situations and help you figure out where you are, how you got there, and where to go next. Therapists do most of this by listening and asking a bunch of questions, and they often do it while you get to play games, do crafts, or fidget with a million awesome fidget toys.

Lots of folks think that going to a therapist means there's something wrong with them. This is not true.

Talking to a therapist just means you haven't found the right BuRPs yet or you need some new strategies for remembering to

BuRP. The therapist will help you figure all of that out.

Other folks think that if you meet with a therapist, you'll have to keep meeting with a therapist forever. This is also false. Some kids only talk to therapists once or twice, while other kids meet with them for a few months or longer. You, your therapist, and your parents will figure out what's right for you!

If you think it might be helpful to talk to a therapist, tell a grown-up you trust. This might be your parents, grandparents, your best friend's parents, your favorite teacher, or the counselor at school. They'll help you figure out what to do next. (And if talking to an adult feels too hard, maybe you can bookmark this page and hand it to them. I bet they'll figure out what you're trying to tell them!)

The Most Important Thing to Remember

Unlike real burps, Button Reduction Practices are always a good choice and you can practice them anywhere, anytime, no matter what.

No matter how often you BuRP, there will still be times when your buttons are pushed and you freak out. That's OK! It doesn't mean you're doing anything wrong or there's anything wrong with you. It's just part of being human. Fortunately, there are things you can do to calm down when you're freaking out anyway, and that's what we're going to talk about next.

Chapter 8

HOW TO
CALM DOWN
AFTER YOU FREAK OUT ANYWAY

N o matter what you do, no matter how often you
BuRP (or don't), no matter how well you avoid
or deal with the button pushers in your life, your buttons
will still be pushed and you're still going to freak out
sometimes.

And that's OK. It really is. You don't have to be perfect to
be awesome and we all lose it sometimes. And when that
happens, the best thing to do is to cut yourself a lot of slack

(meaning, don't beat yourself up!), and do whatever you can to get calm and avoid another freak out.

It just takes three steps: Notice, Breathe, and BuRP.

TRUTH BOMB

It would probably be easier if I could tell you *exactly* how to calm down. Take three deep breaths, touch your toes twice, and repeat, "Cheeky chickens eat cheese in chairs" twelve times fast and you'll be good to go. Wouldn't that be great? Well, only if it actually works for you. But if cheese-eating cheeky chickens stress you out, then that would be terrible advice for calming down. That's why *you* get to pick the BuRP that will help you focus your thoughts, calm your feelings, and take care of your body.

In order to understand how these three steps work, we need to talk about roller coasters. Yes, I said roller coasters, and that's because freaking out is a lot like riding one.

HOW A ROLLER COASTER IS LIKE A FREAK OUT AND WHAT TO DO ABOUT IT

Imagine you're going to an amusement park. Maybe you've been waiting for this all week, or maybe your friend is dragging you. Either way, as you walk through the main entrance, you and your bestie start planning which rides you'll go on. Whether you're excited or freaked out, you've got lots of thoughts and feelings about the day and your buttons are starting to light up.

You decide to go on the roller coaster, so you and your friend get in line. You can see the cars rumbling up the tracks and flying through the turns and loops and you hear the riders screaming. Maybe you're wishing you could push through to the front and get on the ride right now, or maybe you're wondering if you can slowly back away and head over to the carousel without your friend noticing. Your buttons are getting bigger and brighter.

You're almost at the front of the line. You can actually feel the wind from the speeding coaster and you can see the riders' faces—some of them look pretty happy but others are totally freaked out. As for you, you're basically one giant button right now, just waiting to be pushed. Technically, you could still walk away from the ride, but it's pretty hard right now. You've waited a long time, your friend is super excited, and you'd have to shove your way past all the people in line behind you.

When it's finally your turn, you climb into your seat and the ride attendant locks down the safety bar. Maybe you're chomping at the bit to get this ride going, or maybe you're having serious doubts. Technically, you still have one last chance to get off, but you'd have to call the attendant over and pause the ride, everyone would see, and it would cause a whole big scene and that's embarrassing. For better or worse, you feel stuck.

The coaster starts moving, and you start chugging up up up up until you get to the very top of the hill and then . . .

AAAAGGGGGGGGHHHHHHHHHHHH!

If you were psyched to get on this coaster, then you're screaming from happiness and excitement. The thrill is awesome! But if you weren't so thrilled about the coaster, then this is the sound of you freaking out.

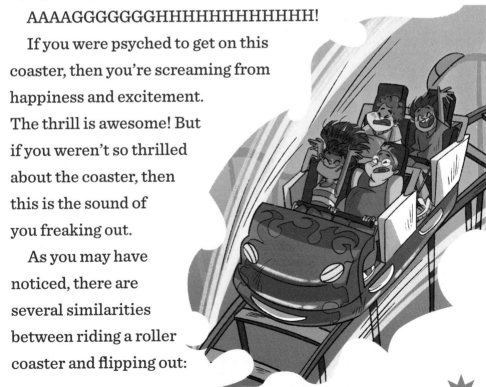

As you may have noticed, there are several similarities between riding a roller coaster and flipping out:

1 the closer you get to either a roller coaster ride or a freak out, the harder it is to switch tracks or calm down,

2 both experiences can feel super intense and out of control, and

3 neither of them last very long.

There are also a lot of differences between an amusement park ride and totally losing your cool, but we're going to focus on the most important one: *you can't get off the coaster once it gets going, but you actually can stop a freak out after it starts.*

You can.

I promise.

It's not always easy, but it's definitely possible.

How? Imagine there was a brake lever on the roller coaster, and all you needed to do was pull on it in order to slow down—or even stop—the ride (aka your freak out). You can do the same thing for a freak out—pull your imaginary brake.

PULL HERE TO CALM DOWN

FUN FREAK OUT FACT

Some roller coasters do have brakes! They're called mountain coasters because they're often built on ski mountains and you can ride them in the summer. On a mountain coaster there are only one or two riders in each car, and the front rider has a brake lever they can pull at any time to slow the ride down. Riders still can't get off the track until they go all the way through the ride, but they can go as slowly as they'd like.

NOTICE, BREATHE, AND BURP

As much as a freak out might seem like an uncontrollable roller coaster ride, the thing to remember is that no matter how intense it feels, you can always pull that brake lever and take back control of your ride. It takes practice, though, and this is where we come back to your easy three-step strategy: **Notice, Breathe, and BuRP.**

STEP 1: NOTICE

You already know that noticing is a powerful BuRP, but now we're going to talk about how noticing can help you avoid or end a freak out. You always have options for calming down, but if you're too caught up in your big feelings and confusing thoughts to notice you're having them, then you can't make the choice to do something that will help you feel better, calmer, and more in control.

TRUTH BOMB

Noticing gives you choices. Noticing gives you the power to decide what you're going to do next.

Fortunately, you can get better at noticing. Lots of folks think noticing is something we just randomly happen to do sometimes, and if we're lucky, we'll notice the right thing at the right time. Like when you happened to notice that your history homework was still sitting on the kitchen table and you grabbed it on your way out the door. Or when your grandpa happened to notice that he'd left his coffee mug on the top of his car and he took it down before he drove off, broke the mug, and spilled coffee all over his windshield.

Those random noticings are great when they happen, but you don't have to leave noticing up to chance or luck. Noticing is a skill that you can get better at with practice. If you've ever plunked around on a piano or played flag football, you know that you might get lucky and hit the right note or snag a flag on your first try, but there's no guarantee it will happen again. But with practice, you'll be able to play an entire song or score a touchdown, even in high-pressure situations like recitals and championship games.

Noticing works the same way. The more you practice noticing, or paying attention to something on purpose, the easier and more natural it becomes—even in high-pressure situations like freak outs. And that's pretty cool.

But what, exactly, are you supposed to notice?

If you're super calm and not anywhere near a flip out, **notice anything you want**! Let's say that instead of standing in line for a roller coaster, you're in line for bumper cars, which you love and do not make you anxious at all. Instead of getting lost in your thoughts about the coaster, take a moment to just look around and notice. What do you see? Hear? Smell? Are you touching anything? Can you taste anything? Maybe you'll notice something awesome—maybe the green car in the corner has a turtle on the hood and you love turtles so you're definitely getting that one. Or maybe you'll notice something annoying, like the loud buzzer announcing the end of the ride.

Or maybe most of what you notice is pretty meh, not awesome or annoying, and that's OK, too. The point is just to practice noticing, which will not only keep you

calm in the moment, but it will also help you get better at noticing so you'll be able to do it when you're about to freak out!

If you're headed toward a freak out (or think you might be headed toward a freak out), **try noticing your tells.** In the card game of poker, a tell is a subtle change in the way a player behaves that might be a clue as to which cards they

TRUTH BOMB

Researchers have found that people report feeling happier when they notice what they're doing (or seeing, hearing, smelling, touching, or tasting) than when they're distracted or thinking about something other than what they're doing.

have and whether they're bluffing (which means lying) about what they have or not. Most poker players aren't even aware of their tells unless someone else points them out. For example, a player might pull on their ear every time they have a great hand or look up at the ceiling when they're bluffing.

When it comes to freak outs, your tells are the thoughts, feelings, and behaviors that you are likely to have or do before you freak out. These tells can give you a clue as to how bright and sensitive your buttons are and how close you are to freaking out. Sometimes your tells are really obvious (maybe you ball up your hands in fists and start snapping at your sister), and sometimes they're more subtle (maybe you notice the tiniest sting of a tear building in the corner of your eye).

Everyone's tells are a little different, and they change over time. The trick is to figure out yours so you'll notice them the next time they happen. Here are a few possible examples:

- Just before you freak out in class, you wish that your new homeroom teacher would get a new job or move down a grade or decide to become a professional scuba diver. **(Thought!)**

- Maybe you find yourself getting angry or anxious just before you lose it with your little brother. **(Feeling!)**

- Maybe you notice that the muscles in your legs are super tight and tense. **(Physical sensation!)**

- Maybe you start tapping your fingers on your desk every time you get annoyed. **(Behavior!)**

You don't have to fix or change or get rid of your tells. Your goal is just to notice them, because when you notice a tell that means your buttons are starting to light up and you might be headed for a freak out. You can choose to breathe and BuRP instead of losing it!

QUICK QUIZ

The closer you are to a freak out, the harder it gets to notice your tells. Why is that? Is it because:

A. When you get really close to exploding, you always close your eyes and jam your fingers in your ears and immediately clear your mind of all thoughts so there's nothing left to notice.

B. The closer you get to melting down, the more brain power is going to the Safety Squirrel limbic system, which doesn't give two hoots about all this noticing nonsense.

C. The closer you get to a freak out, the more likely you are to fall asleep, which makes it really hard to notice anything.

Answer: B! As you get closer to totally exploding, your PFC goes quiet and your limbic system takes over.

If you're already wigging out, **notice something really easy and obvious.** Noticing is hardest to do when you're actively losing it. It might seem like you're trapped on a roller coaster, but remember, you always have a brake you can pull to slow things down. Noticing gives your PFC that little shake it needs to wake up and start figuring out how to calm you down, which slows down your freak out. The trick is to pick something super easy and obvious that's not going to take a lot of PFC power. You can notice that you're freaking out, or that there is a sky above you, or that your feet are touching the ground, or that you have thumbs. Remember: the easier the better. (And whatever you do, don't feel bad if you don't notice your freak outs until they've already passed. That's totally normal, and it will get better with practice!) If you have no idea what's going on, how you're feeling, what you're thinking, or even what day it is, *you can always notice your breath*, which is actually step 2!

STEP 2: BREATHE

Just noticing something—anything—will help calm down your limbic system and power up your PFC, which is the first step toward calming down. The next step is to breathe.

The good news is that you already know how to breathe, and you know why breathing is important—it's that text message directly to your brain and body that everything is OK, and you don't need to freak out. Here are a few other cool facts about breathing:

1 Your breath is always with you. You don't have to go looking for it, you don't need any tools, and you don't have to find something to notice every time you're in a new situation.

2 You can notice your breath anywhere, anytime, totally on the sly. No one has to know what you're doing.

3 Your mind will probably wander, and it might try to freak out again. That's totally normal, and it doesn't mean you're doing anything wrong. Just notice what your brain does and keep on breathing.

Remember, you can breathe however you'd like to! You don't have to breathe faster or slower or hold your breath or breathe in a certain way. Having said that, here are a few different options you can try:

• Focus on how your breath feels in your body. You can notice your belly moving in and out (or up and down if you're lying down), or the way your breath feels moving in and out of your mouth, or how it feels as you inhale and exhale through your nose.

• Count your breaths. Inhale – one, exhale – two, inhale – three, exhale – four, and so on. You can count up to eight or ten or whatever your favorite number is, and then start back at one.

- Say (or think) "in" each time you breathe in and say (or think) "out" each time you breathe out. Repeat.

STEP 3: BURP

By now you know that BuRPs are great for calming down your buttons. What you might not know is that they work in any stage of a freak out—way before it happens, right before it happens, while it's happening, and yes, even afterward when you're trying to chill out instead of flipping out.

You have at least twenty-six different BuRPs at your disposal already (see pages 94 to 105). The trick to BuRPing well is picking the right BuRP for the right time. Here are a few tips to remember when you're coming out of an explosion and hoping to avoid another one:

- The best BuRP is the one you can do in that moment. If you've just lost it in gym class, you might not be able to practice your favorite hobby or quack like a duck. But maybe you can grab a quick drink of water, stretch your body, remember your favorite song lyrics, or count backward from one hundred.

TRUTH BOMB

Noticing your breath is a great strategy for lots of folks, but not everyone. If you have asthma or any problems with breathing, then you might prefer to notice something else. No problem! Other options include counting to ten over and over again, wearing a beaded bracelet, or keeping a smooth stone in your pocket that you can notice and touch whenever you need to.

• BuRPs that keep you calm instead of freaking out may not be the same ones that help you calm down after you've already lost it. Some people need to move their bodies, while others need to stay still. Some folks want to be alone after a freak out, while others prefer to be with trusted friends or family members. You might need to experiment with a few different options before you find the one that's right for you, and that's OK!

• It might be hard to remember what to do when you're trying to calm down. Try making a list of your favorite BuRPs and leaving it on your dresser, in your backpack, or anywhere you're likely to see it after a freak out. Just reading the list might be enough to help you calm down!

• Remember, anything that relaxes your body, focuses your thoughts, and calms your feelings is a great way to get back on track after a meltdown.

Notice, Breathe, and BuRP.

That's your super simple strategy for calming down at any stage of any freak out. What you notice, how you breathe, and what you BuRP might look different for different freak outs, and that's totally cool. Also, the notice, breathe, and BuRP strategy might not always feel easy or feel like it's working. Even if it's not working perfectly, I promise it's the best thing to do to try to calm down. And sometimes you might completely forget to do it. That's totally normal! The more you practice, the easier and more natural it will be.

The Most Important Thing to Remember

Any time you're freaking out, you might be freaking out, or you think you might be freaking out is a great time to Notice, Breathe, and BuRP.

So now it's time to put it all together!

Chapter 9

PUTTING IT ALL TOGETHER

We've talked about a lot in this book—why you freak out, how to get to know your buttons and make them less pushable, and what to do after you freak out anyway, not to mention F.A.R.T.s, BuRPS, Safety Squirrels, and roller coasters. It's a lot to remember! Here are some quick quiz questions to help you pull it all together.

128

Your parents just told you that your annual checkup at the doctor's office is next week, and you know what that means. Shots. You hate shots. Despise them. Just thinking about them makes you feel tense and anxious and scared and you basically become one huge glowing button, just begging to be pushed. ZOINKS!

1 **In the days before your doctor's appointment, should you:**

A. Try to remember, in as much detail as possible, exactly how much your past vaccinations have hurt so you'll know what to expect.

B. Talk about it all as often as you can, with as many people as you can. Tell everyone you know how much you hate getting injections and how freaked out you are.

C. Notice, as often as you can, when your buttons are bright, glowing, and super pushable. Focus on your breathing whenever you start feeling upset and practice your BuRPs as often as you can.

D. Try to convince your parents that you really, really don't need your vaccinations. Make a slideshow presentation if you have to.

2 You're at the doctor's office and you see the syringes on the counter. Your belly clenches up and you can hardly breathe. Your mom hands you your headphones and turns on your favorite song. Eventually the moment passes, but you still have to get three shots, and you're still feeling super tense. Should you:

A. Make a grab for the syringes and throw them down the garbage chute.

B. Ask to go to the bathroom, and then sprint down the hall, out of the office, and straight back to the car.

C. Go boneless, slither to the floor, and refuse to get up until your mom and the doctor both promise you don't have to get any more injections ever for the rest of eternity.

D. Notice that you're still upset, take a deep breath, and recite the mantra you practiced with your mom before the appointment: "I can handle this. I can handle this."

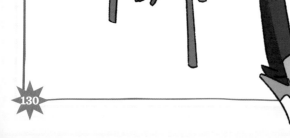

Hopefully that was the easiest pop quiz you've ever taken.

Notice, Breathe, and BuRP is your go-to strategy at any stage of the freak-out process, and it's your best shot at getting through difficult moments in the easiest way possible.

HOW TO STOP FREAKING OUT IN THREE EASY STEPS

1 Notice that you're freaking out. If you're not sure what to notice, C.A.L.M. will help you check in with your body, W.A.I.T. will focus your thoughts, and Name It to Tame It is a great way to calm down your feelings. You can also notice that the walls are white and the grass is green—anything works as long as you're noticing it.

2 Breathe. That's all you have to do. Just breathe. Bonus points if you notice you're breathing.

3 BuRP. When you're freaking out, easy BuRPs are great choices. Keep breathing, take some slow, deep breaths, do some jumping jacks, head outside for a minute, count to ten, or whatever works for you.

The Most Important Thing to Remember

No matter what happens, no matter how bonkers or out of control your freak out is or was, cut yourself a whole lotta slack. Being human is hard. Everyone makes mistakes and goes bonkers sometimes and that's OK. Cutting yourself some slack means forgiving yourself and being kind to yourself when you freak out. It means trying not to beat yourself up for being less than perfect, remembering that nobody is perfect, and you don't have to be perfect to be awesome.

Keep noticing and breathing and BuRPing. You got this. You're doing great.

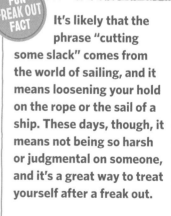

FUN FREAK OUT FACT It's likely that the phrase "cutting some slack" comes from the world of sailing, and it means loosening your hold on the rope or the sail of a ship. These days, though, it means not being so harsh or judgmental on someone, and it's a great way to treat yourself after a freak out.

RESOURCES

If you'd like to learn more about how to freak out less, talking to a trusted adult is a great place to start. You could check in with a family member like a parent, grandparent, aunt, or uncle. Or it might feel better to talk to someone outside your family, like a therapist, counselor, teacher, coach, minister, rabbi, or imam.

If you'd prefer to keep reading, your local library is a great resource. If you can't find the book you're looking for, ask the librarian. Librarians love to help kids find books!

In addition, here are a few books you might like:

How to Master Your Mood in Middle School: Kid Confident Book 2 by Lenka Glassman (Magination Press, 2022)

How to Handle Stress for Middle School Success: Kid Confident Book 3 by Silvi Guerra (Magination Press, 2023)

Coping Skills for Kids Workbook by Janine Halloran (PESI Publishing & Media, 2018)

Outsmarting Worry: An Older Kid's Guide to Managing Anxiety by Dawn Huebner (Jessica Kingsley Publishers, 2017)

Something Bad Happened: A Kid's Guide to Coping with Events in the News by Dawn Huebner (Jessica Kingsley Publishers, 2019)

Superpowered: Transform Anxiety into Courage, Confidence, and Resilience by Renee Jain and Dr. Shefali Tsabary (Random House Books for Young Readers, 2020)

Why Do I Feel So Worried?: A Kid's Guide to Coping with Big Emotions by Tammi Kirkness (The Experiment, 2022)

The Tween Book: A Growing-Up Guide for the Changing You by Wendy L. Moss and Donald A. Moses (Magination Press, 2015)

Guy Stuff Feelings: Everything You Need to Know About Your Emotions by Cara Natterson (American Girl, 2021)

How To Be a Person: 65 Hugely Useful, Super-Important Skills to Learn before You're Grown Up by Catherine Newman (Storey Publishing, 2020)

Psychology for Kids: The Science of the Mind and Behavior by Jacqueline B. Toner and Claire A. B. Freeland (Magination Press, 2021)

How to Take the Grrrr Out of Anger by Elizabeth Verdick and Marjorie Lisovskis (Free Spirit Publishing, 2015)

Your Happiest You: The Care & Keeping of Your Mind and Spirit by Judy Woodburn (American Girl, 2017)

ABOUT THE AUTHOR

CARLA NAUMBURG, PhD, LICSW, is a clinical social worker and the author of four parenting books, including one about how parents can freak out less. Carla's favorite hobbies are reading (especially mysteries!), cross-stitching, hiking, and hanging out with her cats, Gittel and Gertie. She lives in Massachusetts with her husband and daughters.

ABOUT THE ILLUSTRATOR

LETIZIA RIZZO is a freelance illustrator based in Lecce, Italy. She has worked with numerous publishers, including Cottage Door Press, Oxford University Press, Hachette, Sterling Publishing, Little Bee Books, Scholastic, HarperCollins, and others.